ZEN
IN YOUR GARDEN

ZEN
IN YOUR GARDEN

Jenny Hendy

TUTTLE PUBLISHING
BOSTON • RUTLAND, VERMONT • TOKYO

For Jim and Jenny

with love

The publisher would like to thank Godsfield Press and the author for their kind permission to reproduce the poems and quotes from *Zen Wisdom,* © 1998 Timothy Freke, and *Taoist Wisdom,* © 1999 Timothy Freke. The quotes on pages 17, 65, and 105 are from *Zen Speaks: Shouts of Nothingness,* an Anchor Book, published by Doubleday, a division of Bantam Doubleday Dell Publishing Group, Inc.

First published in the United States in 2001 by Tuttle Publishing, an imprint of Periplus Editions (HK) Ltd, with editorial offices at 153 Milk Street, Boston, Massachusetts 02109.

Text copyright © 2001 Jenny Hendy

Library of Congress Cataloging-in-Publication Data
Hendy, Jenny, 1961-
  Zen in your garden / Jenny Hendy.--1st ed.
    p.cm.
  ISBN 0-8048-3289-7 (hc)
    1. Gardens, Japanese--Zen influences.   I. Title.
  SB458. H43 2001
  712.6'0952--dc21

ISBN: 0-8048-3289-7

Designer: Justina Leitão
Editor: Jane Alexander
Illustrations: Coral Mula
In-house editor: Katey Day
Design © Godsfield Press

Distributed by

North America
Tuttle Publishing, Distribution Center, Airport Industrial Park
364 Innovation Drive, North Clarendon, VT 05759-9436
Tel: (802) 773-8930
Tel: (800) 526-2778
Fax: (802) 773-6993

Japan
Tuttle Publishing, RK Building, 2nd Floor
2-13-10 Shimo-Meguro, Meguro-Ku, Tokyo 153 0064
Tel: (03) 5437-0171
Fax: (03) 5437-0755

Asia Pacific
Berkeley Books Pte Ltd, 5 Little Road #08-0
Singapore 536983
Tel: (65) 280-1330
Fax: (65) 280-6290

1 3 5 7 9 10 8 6 4 2
07 06 05 04 03 02 01

Printed in Singapore

Contents

Beginning with Zen

Spring flowers, autumn moon,
Summer breeze, winter snow—
When the *mind* is free
From unnecessary thoughts
Every season is just *perfect*

Now more than ever, in our increasingly complex and rapidly changing society, we feel the need for tranquility and harmony, and the East may provide the inspiration we need to simplify our lives, to "clear the clutter," not only from our surroundings, but also from our minds. Faced with more and more technological innovation, the desire to step back into the natural world grows, and the garden is often regarded as a sanctuary.

Introduction

The Zen Buddhist monastery gardens of Kyoto generate a profound atmosphere of serenity. This book seeks to explain some of the guiding principles and philosophies of Zen in the hope that we, too, can create a garden with a similar feeling of peace and tranquility. It also looks at what Zen can teach us about how we might approach the garden and the way to work within it.

It is not the result of our *actions*
That we are *working* for, but the
Fulfillment of just *doing*

THE ZEN WAY

The Japanese esthetic that evolved from Zen Buddhism is one of extreme simplicity. It gave birth to the Minimalist movement in the West, but this is often seen purely as a design concept and has lost its spiritual and symbolic aspect. This book is about following the Zen way. It is not a blueprint for creating a replica of a Japanese garden, even if that

were possible. It takes a Zen master many years to learn his art, and make no mistake, Japanese gardening is an art form.

SPACE AND SIMPLICITY

The dry gardens constructed from rock and gravel are too austere for some tastes. We are used to the notion that a space has to be filled with flowers and foliage before it can be termed a garden. However, in the Zen garden, the space is an integral part of the design.

Zen-garden style evolved over a long period in Japan, but it has remained virtually unchanged for centuries. When monks teaching Zen Buddhism first came to Japan from mainland China and Korea, their austere approach was rejected by the ruling imperial classes; but when the military later took over Zen Buddhism found favor. The monks brought with them Chinese paintings of rugged mountain peaks and waterfalls, and these stark black-ink images influenced the design of the monastery gardens. Taoism and aspects of Shinto, a form of nature worship and the prevailing religion in Japan, also found its way into Zen.

TRADITIONAL GARDENS

Zen monastic gardens usually occupy a rectangular courtyard with a backdrop of plain walls and perhaps a wooden veranda from which to view the raked gravel and rock compositions. The gravel must be raked, cleaned, and weeded; and the moss and other plantings that surround the rock groupings require careful tending. The monks do this as part of their daily routine, and interestingly, it is the senior monks and Zen masters who do the most

above: This contemporary garden combines dressed stone with natural boulders. The bamboo deer-scarer is a traditional water feature.

tedious and arduous work. These are not meditation gardens, but they are designed for contemplation and provide a quiet setting for the monks' spiritual way of life. We can adapt the monastic style, creating spaces for contemplation and meditation in our own gardens, so long as we stay true to the basic principles of Zen.

Certain elements characterize the Japanese arts and are an integral part of Zen garden design. In the West, the approach to garden creation is quite different.

Japanese Esthetics

MINIMALISM

When deciding what changes to make to your garden, keep in mind the very powerful phrase "less is more." The question you might ask yourself is "what can I leave out?" rather than "how much more can I cram in?" The garden can be seen as a metaphor for your own life—keep only what you need, the rest is superfluous.

The minimalist approach applies to all aspects of gardening. The overall design should have smooth, clean lines and no unnecessary flourishes. The detail of hard landscaping and planting should also follow minimalist principles. With so few elements chosen and placed so carefully, the rest of the garden becomes a harmonious space—a sea of emptiness.

In the Zen garden the palette is extremely restricted so that the senses are soothed rather than stimulated. Reducing the number of colors also has the effect of making you aware of just how many subtle shades of green there really are. With a backdrop of cool leafiness, grays, and soft earth tones, a sense of peace pervades the garden. There are no flower beds with myriad shades and forms jostling for attention. Instead, when a single bloom opens against a verdant backcloth or when petals fall to the ground, the contrasting color becomes a point of real focus.

Let everything go

Where it naturally wants to go

And you will *always*

be *successful*

ASYMMETRY AND MOVEMENT

In the West, the Classical style was typified by symmetry, and even today formal gardens are usually based on repeated geometric shapes. But symmetry is extremely rare in Zen gardens. It is never observed in the natural landscape, and Japanese gardens strive to represent features of the countryside, even if it is only symbolic.

right: *The simplicity and rhythm of this design, which combines natural and man-made elements, is the key to its success.*

Formal gardens are often designed around a central axis, which tends to result in a static composition, but many Eastern cultures believe it is important to keep the flow of energy, or chi, that unites all things moving freely within a space. In Japan this energy is known as ki. You only have to look at the curve of a stepping-stone path, which leads the eye to some distant point, to appreciate the fluidity in design of a well-made Japanese garden.

BALANCE

In Zen gardens the various elements remain in perfect harmony with one another. Balance is exemplified by the symbol for yin and yang, or in and yo as they are called in Japan, the two opposing forces in nature. The black and white halves are mirror images making up the whole, but in each

above: Where there is harmony, yin and yang are perfectly balanced. Notice that each contains a tiny amount of the other's nature.

left: A mown path winds its way in broad sweeping curves through a wildflower meadow, allowing energy to flow with ease.

half there is a tiny spot of the other's color, symbolizing that one simply cannot exist without the other, that yin and yang are inseparable.

In the garden, yin is represented by sand and gravel because these symbolize the yin element of water. This is balanced by the yang elements of rock and plants. A careful balance is maintained between opposing forces. For instance, in rock or plant groupings, vertical shapes, which are yang, are set against low horizontal shapes, which are yin; light, sunny areas (yang) are complemented by cool shady areas (yin); and the rustle of bamboo leaves (yang) is contrasted by silence (yin).

In Zen gardens, individual rock groupings are carefully arranged to create a harmonious shape, usually a triangle. With its wide base the triangle is essentially very stable, and it therefore generates a feeling of restfulness. It is also symbolic of the mountain whose "roots" go deep underground. In the Zen garden stability and balance are so important that rocks are literally part-buried in the ground.

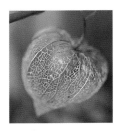

One of the basic precepts of Zen is to live life in the moment, to be truly alive and aware right now, without diverting ourselves with thoughts of either the past or the future. Following this path, it is ultimately possible to realize your true potential, releasing creative energy you never knew you had.

The Zen Approach

MINDFULNESS

There is a wonderful story of a Zen monk responding to someone boasting about his own accomplishments. The monk replied that his master was also a very talented and developed man, because he, too, could perform the most astonishing feats. For instance, if he slept, he slept, and if he ate, he ate. This is the essence of mindfulness: to do one thing with your full concentration, whether it be weeding or watering, spreading fertilizer or pruning a shrub. This exercise in concentration is a kind of active meditation. It is very calming to work in this way, helping to soothe frayed nerves, lower blood pressure, and to generate a feeling of well-being. The mindful gardener learns to be more focused and less easily distracted, and develops powers of observation. The most subtle changes occurring in the garden are observed in minute detail—the pattern of leaf shadows, morning dew on petals—and time seems to pass more slowly.

SYMBOLISM

The dry garden is perhaps the most extreme example of symbolism in Zen gardening. On one level the rock and moss groupings could represent islands surrounded by a lake, or mountain peaks emerging through the cloud layer. At a deeper level, the rocks could represent individual thoughts arising out of a sea of mind—the ripples and eddies suggested by the raked patterns symbolizing disturbances in the mind created by these thoughts. Most gardens are too small to include a life-sized replica of a mountain torrent, but on a smaller scale the skilled Zen gardener can create the impression of a waterfall using carefully chosen and positioned rocks.

Once you start to view the garden as symbolic, you begin to draw inspiration from it in many different ways: a pond, for instance, might be viewed as the entire world in microcosm.

SACRED ELEMENTS

Zen regards the whole universe as sacred. You can embrace the philosophy of Zen whatever your religious persuasion. There is no reason why you could not use a symbol of your own faith as a point of focus in the garden. Whatever you choose, it should be sited carefully and treated with reverence and respect. In Japanese homes, a large niche or *tokonoma* is often used to display a few beautifully arranged flowers or a scroll painting, or even to house a small shrine.

Age and endurance correlate to wisdom in Japan. This is why old, gnarled, and windblown trees are revered and why plants such as bonsai are trained to look older than they are. Weathered rocks covered in mosses and lichens are also sought after, and a patina of age is considered desirable.

In a certain *sense*
Zen is feeling life
Instead of feeling
Something about *life*

WORKING WITH NATURE

We are like caretakers in the garden and should tread carefully lest we harm any creature. In Zen, even supposed pests have a right to our respect and compassion. This means that organic gardening methods are likely to be followed. We may encourage all kinds of wildlife to share the garden, and if we have achieved a balance, because we have looked after the soil and given plants the conditions they need, then no "visitor" should be a problem.

above left: This Chinese lantern—a gemstone in a casing of filigree gold—reminds us of the beauty and fragility of nature.

right: The serene figure of a stone-carved Buddha helps focus the mind on more spiritual matters.

Many of the techniques for creating the illusion of space that have been perfected in Japanese gardens over centuries can be applied in Western gardens, making the most of small urban plots and even tiny courtyards and roof terraces.

Leading the Eye

FALSE PERSPECTIVE

To create an illusion of length in the garden, plants and screens can be layered between the viewer and the garden boundary in the same way that a three-dimensional effect of depth is created with scenery at the theater. This makes it impossible to see the whole garden from one viewpoint. Larger, brighter plants can used for foreground planting and progressively smaller, more subdued plants as you move farther away. Foliage size also decreases with distance. To increase the illusion of length, paths can also be tapered so they become narrower as they wind away from the house. For example, a stepping stone pathway could use larger pieces of flat rock at the start, leaving plenty of space all around. As the path travels down the garden, the pieces used are smaller and closer together, with the planting brought closer to funnel the pathway and gradually conceal sections of it.

When the distance from the house to the opposite boundary is relatively short, it is important that the lines of pathways and planting curve across the space to make the eye travel along a diagonal line. This takes the emphasis away from the opposite boundary line and makes the garden feel longer. A strong focus in direct line with the house should be avoided; this foreshortens the view.

BORROWED LANDSCAPE

Known as *shakkei* in Japan, this is where part of the landscape beyond the garden is incorporated into the scene by framing the view. The garden appears to run on seamlessly to the far point in the distance because the real boundary is carefully screened. In Japan, boundaries are screened with planting, by using the natural contouring of the ground, and sometimes by clipped hedging. In a rural setting it is relatively easy to incorporate views of the surrounding countryside, but in urban situations, distant views need to be chosen with care and sensitivity—selectively framing certain parts and blocking out less pleasant aspects.

FILTERING AND FRAMING THE VIEW

Depending on where you are within the garden or house, certain elements may be deliberately framed to create a picture for the viewer. That scene may

right: A glimpse of blue water—narrowly framed views of an intriguing scene make us keen to explore further.

only be noticed from certain angles, such as when you are sitting as opposed to standing, and so on. There is a wonderful story of a Zen tea master, who created a garden for a tea house, which had panoramic views of Japan's Inland Sea. Guests were puzzled by the fact that he had planted two tall hedges, deliberately blocking out the beautiful view from the garden. It was only in the act of ritual purification, when one of the participants of the tea ceremony knelt down to scoop up water from the stone basin, that he caught a glimpse of the sea though a small gap. In a moment of realization he understood that the water in his hands and the limitless ocean were the same and that mind and the Infinite were one also.

However much we desire privacy, it is probably a mistake to try to block out the world entirely— we may inadvertently turn the garden into a dark and claustrophobic space rather than a sanctuary.

In *nature* you already own

The stars, the moon,

mountains

Most divisions within the garden can be created using light screens and airy planting to baffle the eye, causing it to focus on the screen itself and the foreground planting, rather than on the area beyond. However, solid divisions may be appropriate when creating a quiet and private area for contemplation or meditation, when complete seclusion might be helpful. Most traditional monastery gardens are walled for this reason.

part two

Design

A cluster of summer *trees*

A *glimpse* of the sea

A pale evening *moon*

A Modern Interpretation

You could say that the house is the single largest "feature" in the garden. Plain buildings, particularly modern architecture with strong rectilinear lines, make an excellent backdrop for a Zen dry garden. The simplicity of both forms means that they fit together without conflict. In certain parts of the world, this kind of architecture is common for dwellings. Elsewhere, minimalist architecture tends to be confined to office buildings.

There is potential conflict in creating a traditional Japanese garden in the West, because the garden style may clash with the architecture. The overall design and layout and the traditional features and ornaments found within the Japanese garden are instantly recognizable as coming from that culture. Happily, the Zen garden does not have to be recognizably Japanese.

CREATING A SETTING

The style of house becomes less of a problem if the garden is oriented away from the building. It is sometimes possible to blend the walls in with the garden by making a façade for the building which helps it to disappear into the background—a combination of planting and application of a wooden framework, for example. You could also create a screen of shrubs and trees a short distance away, so the house is partially masked when viewed from the garden.

If the house presents no problems as a backdrop, but unsuitable architecture and unpleasant outlooks surround the plot, you could establish a boundary that encapsulates the garden so that little of the

left: Still very much designed around Zen principles, this ultramodern courtyard garden is at once dramatic and restful.

outside world is visible. In a small plot it is good to see some open sky, even if you compromise and keep some of the surrounding rooflines, too.

Follow your own light
Be ordinary
Then you will *see* for yourself
That you are part
of the *whole*

Another possibility is to make a garden within a garden—creating a traditional Japanese garden room with its own green enclosure, perhaps formed by clipped hedging. This could be your sanctuary garden—a place for meditation and contemplation, where you can leave behind your day-to-day world and enter a more spiritual realm. A less rigid approach is to take elements of the design and philosophy of Zen gardens and work them into an existing landscape, blending the two cultures in a way that enhances the whole.

21

One way to facilitate the blending of East and West is to source locally available materials. The white sand or grit used in the temple gardens in Kyoto is used partly because it is readily available there. We could use gravel from the local pit.

Adapting Local Materials

SIMPLE DECORATIVE ELEMENTS

If you want to add an overtly Japanese-styled element to your design, you will find ornaments such as reproduction stone lanterns are readily available, although the quality varies tremendously. In

Zen gardens, very plain, simple, man-made objects or natural materials work best. You might introduce a large, undecorated terracotta or stoneware jar, a modern sculpture, or a large piece of driftwood. A stone-effect trough, the sort usually made from cast concrete and designed for alpine gardening, could also be adapted to make a water-basin feature.

Voids or open spaces can be surfaced with good-quality reproduction stone paving, concrete, or wooden decking to create flat expanses in place of gravel. Very good alternatives to granite blocks are available and can be used for edging and for paths.

MOSS SUBSTITUTES

In Japan, moss frequently features in gardens, but it does not grow easily unless conditions are sufficiently moist and shady (Japan has a very high

annual rainfall). In a well-lit and well-drained area, you could use close-mown grass instead.

STONE

Many Zen gardens are characterized by large pieces of stone. Quarried stone can be very expensive and is hard to transport and maneuver, but it does enhance the garden. Artificial rock, such as can be found in water-garden suppliers, rarely looks like the real thing. However, you can mix cement on site and sculpt it into smooth organic shapes. You could certainly use this versatile and convenient material to create a shallow flight of steps, or several large stepping stones set into gravel. When a relatively weak mixture is blended with gravel and pieces of stone or pebbles, it weathers reasonably quickly; the pieces of stone gradually appear as the surface is walked over, giving an interesting aged appearance. The addition of a little peat encourages colonization by algae, lichen, and moss.

SCREENING

Bamboo poles for the construction of screens and fences are now easy to obtain, and split bamboo fencing is available in rolls or ready-made panels. Specialist companies will also supply it by mail. But bamboo has a markedly Eastern feel, so you need to think carefully before incorporating

left: *This group of smooth pebbles, some with interesting veining, could be used as textural detailing in the Zen garden.*

above: *In this modern interpretation of Zen design, rounded boulders and pebbles are replaced with glass and metallic spheres.*

it into your garden. Ordinary square trellis panels, appropriately painted or stained, can be used as a substitute for lashed bamboo screens. Another excellent fencing material is made from split hazel twigs or willow. This woven screening has a beautiful natural texture and color and is ideal as a backdrop for planting.

NEW MATERIALS

All kinds of exciting materials could be used in a modern Zen garden. You could surface an area with recycled glass chips instead of gravel, and in places pile it up to create surreal cones. Glass bricks can be used to make a screen wall or garden divide, and a water feature could be made from polished stainless steel, chrome, or sculpted glass.

Whether you choose the natural, organic look or an ultramodern feel, make the lines clean and simple, in keeping with Zen philosophy. Be very careful about mixing naturalistic and modernistic elements.

Thought Before Action

Think of a master scroll painter. He sits and contemplates the paper, and then suddenly he moves. The brush strokes are swift and positive. Mind and body are in perfect harmony. All the thinking has already been done, and the artist paints with economy and efficiency of movement. Few brush strokes are used, yet the picture has all the necessary elements. Our minds are able to fill in the blanks. So it can be with the Zen garden.

PLANNING THE GARDEN

The monks who created the inspirational monastery gardens of Kyoto would have done so only after a great deal of contemplation, not to mention hard work. It would be folly to think that creating a Zen garden is something you could do over a weekend. It may take several seasons to decide exactly what you want to do. Learn to trust your instincts and to let go when designing—that way, the design will come though in a natural way, from your intuitive self, without the preconceptions and restraints that your conscious mind will try to impose. By designing in this way and by doing the bulk of the construction, the planting, and the tending yourself, you will truly own the garden.

LIVING WITH THE SPACE

Whether building on a brand-new site or adapting an existing garden, you need to experience the space and try to visualize how it will work and how the various elements will combine. Are there any problem areas, and if so, how will they be accommodated? What about the levels? Do you need to add soil or move it elsewhere to create the necessary contouring? What needs to be taken out and what elements retained? Think very carefully before removing any mature shrub specimens or trees, which make the garden feel older and more established. It can take years to achieve the same effect!

Who will use the garden and in what way? How will you accommodate the car, tools, a child's sand pile, and so on? Where are the main viewpoints and how will various areas of the garden be framed?

left: It takes sensitivity and careful consideration to construct a garden such as this. Proper planning supports the creative process.

Where are the entrance and exit points to be located? Are there any elements beyond the garden boundary that could be incorporated into the scene, such as a large tree or a piece of interesting architecture? Stand with your back to the house and look into the garden—try to visualize how it might appear from the house at different times of the year and at different times of day. Do you know where the sun rises and sets? The more you increase your awareness of your site, the happier you will be with your design.

When everything is working *naturally*, The *heart* spontaneously responds With the appropriate *action*

Try out your ideas before committing yourself. A large vase could be expensive, so make sure it will look right in the position you have selected by substituting a cardboard box to check scale and positioning first. Use bamboo stakes lashed together with string to see how wooden constructions might work, and inflate trash bags to model as rocks in your proposed site. Mark the line of pathways using large nails or wooden stakes connected by twine, then live with the design for a period of time to make sure it feels right to you.

Is there anything more
miraculous than the
wonders of nature?
Yes, your appreciation of
those *wonders*

Awakening to the Garden

It is vitally important that you can get out into the garden at all times of year so you can remain grounded and in contact with nature and the earth itself. This oneness with life, with the whole universe, is a fundamental part of Zen. Only with daily forays into the garden will you notice the subtle, fleeting changes and stay in touch with what is going on.

Try keeping a garden diary to record your observations, thoughts, and realizations. Making your walk something of a daily ritual allows a few moments of peace and quiet for reflection and contemplation. Set aside part of each day as your own—even if life is extremely full and hectic, a walk before breakfast or when you come home from work will do wonders for your state of mind. If you can move easily around the garden, you can even make the route into a walking meditation. Being able to walk barefoot on the grass is especially grounding. Night access is as important as dawn and dusk or daytime. In Zen, the moon is a symbol of pure mind, and it is inspiring to see the moon reflected in water on a still, cloudless night.

above: *Gradually, during the course of a morning, this red poppy unfurled its petals. Take time to observe these fleeting moments.*

right: *Under a full moon the garden is bathed in silvery light. Candles and lanterns produce a similarly evocative effect.*

NIGHTTIME

Of course the garden needs to be safe to negotiate at night and some form of lighting will be needed to guide the way, to highlight changes in level and so on. In Zen gardens, stone lanterns traditionally held oil lamps, and lighting the garden with these is an option, though you need to prepare the garden before nightfall unless you do not mind finding your way with a flashlight. Electric lighting is not nearly as evocative as candlelight, but there is such a choice of lighting available now, with subtle effects, that it should certainly be considered. Also do not forget that, when lit at night, the garden will provide a lovely view from inside the house.

OUTDOOR LIVING

A roofed area within the garden is useful when the weather is bad. You could even build a covered walkway. Traditionally, many of the dry monastery gardens of rock and raked gravel were not intended to be walked in and were built in a central courtyard that could be viewed from a veranda. A room with patio doors that open out onto the garden will provide a similar setting.

A Zen garden is a tranquil place for sitting, standing, or walking, and if you wish to meditate, it is ideal for getting yourself into the right mindset, although in truth it does not matter whether you meditate in the garden or inside the house.

The threshold between house and garden is a wonderful place to sit and relax or contemplate, and sliding glass doors allow fresh air and the sounds of the garden into the house. A conservatory or sunroom is another excellent halfway-house between garden and home. Maybe you have a little wooden shed down at the end of the garden that could be converted into an all-weather retreat, perhaps by adding a simple veranda. Provide electricity, and you will even be able to make a hot drink!

In good weather, it is nice to have a place in the garden where you can sit in comfort and without distraction—a green, shady corner next to a pool with a wooden armchair perhaps. The images and atmosphere you absorb will help soothe and calm the mind. Even just a few moments of quiet contemplation before returning to your chores can work wonders for your health and well-being.

Dry Mountain Water

Kare-san-sui has two translations. In one it means "dry mountain water," and conjures up images from the *sansui-ga* black-ink paintings of mountainous scenery and waterfalls that were characteristic of the Muromachi period. *San-sui* or *senzui* also means "garden," so *kare-san-sui* can just mean "garden without water." Whatever the exact meaning, the stylized rock and gravel gardens that are so characteristic of Zen are undoubtedly symbolic.

Through the ages, rock has been a constant feature in Japanese gardens. Shinto considered some rocks to be sacred, and they were garlanded with holy ropes. Some were thought to be the home of spirits, and certain shapes were believed to be auspicious. Today, Zen gardeners are still very much aware of the energy, or *ki* contained in natural rock, and the flow and direction of that *ki* can be felt by a master gardener. The older and more weathered the rock, the more *ki* will have been accumulated, which is why water-worn pieces and rocks covered with lichen and moss are so highly prized. Rocks from the sites of old shrines or temples have also accumulated beneficial *ki*.

SYMBOLIC ELEMENTS

Rock is yang in nature and is balanced by the yin element of water. In the dry garden, water is represented instead by carefully raked grit or fine gravel. These two elements also demonstrate another fundamental relationship—the one that links the Buddhist concept of *ku,* meaning emptiness

left: Raked gravel patterns emphasize the flow of energy, and rock and gravel are in harmony in this contemporary dry garden.

or non-substantiality, with *shinnyo*, meaning suchness or thusness—the true nature of things. In the *kare-san-sui*, an expanse of raked sand is a void, a sea of emptiness. In representing mutable, flowing water, it also expresses impermanence, which is another face of *ku*. By contrast, solid, immovable rock perfectly exemplifies *shinnyo*. Contemplating the rock groupings in a dry garden, we may become fully aware of their existence, and in a flash of inspiration and understanding we may conclude simply that—rock *is*.

There is a similarity between the large areas of white space in the black-and-white Chinese paintings that influenced Zen garden design and the broad, empty expanses of sand in the garden. In both cases, the voids allow the viewer mentally to enter into the creative process, to fill in the gaps in their own way. The dry garden may be thought of as a visual koan, a riddle posed by a master to aid his student's progress in meditation. Contemplating the dry garden, we are drawn out of ourselves; time can appear to stand still, and with practice we move into the void and in so doing enter a higher plane of consciousness.

The interpretation of the rocks is left to the individual. Whether they see rocks, gravel, and plants or something more profound not only depends on their ability to interpret abstract art and their understanding of the "vocabulary" of Zen dry gardens, but also the level of their spiritual development. Setting such matters aside, there is no denying the profound sense of peace experienced after visiting the absolute simplicity and perfection of gardens such as those at Ryoan-ji and Daisen-in.

On one level, the elements of the dry garden combine to create a pleasing composition, the rocks providing rhythm and modulation. The overall shape of the rock groupings and the way that upright rocks are sometimes deliberately tilted can create a sense of flow, emphasized by the lines and patterns raked into the gravel. Each rock, and the way that each grouping is composed, is perfectly balanced when seen from any direction.

Symbolic Rock

On another level, dry gardens have surreal or symbolic qualities, or they may be allegorical. The "islands" of rock surrounded by "water" could be seen as mountain peaks emerging through the cloud layer, and when contemplating the scene you could imagine yourself seated at the pinnacle of a very high mountain. They could also be interpreted as individual thoughts or emotions disturbing the calm sea that is mind, the raking of the gravel indicating the ripples and refractions that such thoughts create. Some dry gardens are recognizably landscapes in miniature, but with highly minimalist, abstract designs, that interpretation becomes more tenuous. The distinction between the viewer and the scene that is viewed becomes blurred, and the mind is free to contemplate the limitless nature of the absolute.

Mount Fuji is often represented in dry gardens in Japan, and you may also find Mount Sumeru (known in Japan as Mount Shumisen), the mythical mountain at the center of the Buddhist cosmology. The number seven is frequently used in the formation of rock groupings; this may be linked to the seven mountain ranges and seven seas, which, according to certain texts, surround the mountain.

Chinese mythology has also been influential, with mythical isles carried on the backs of turtles being depicted in pools and gardens.

CLASSIC CONFIGURATIONS

One particular rock configuration, the *sanzon*, symbolically depicts a number of different scenes. It consists of a tall upright rock, called the water-falling stone, which is surmounted by two subordinate rocks. In addition to symbolizing Mount Sumeru, the *sanzon* may also be used to describe the Buddhist trinity—the Buddha or enlightened one; dharma, the universal truth or his teachings; and *sanga*, the Buddhist community and followers. A further interpretation emphasizes the essential relationship between heaven, earth, and man.

DRY GARDEN IMAGERY

In ordinary homes in Japan, especially in urban areas, a dry garden is most frequently designed to evoke a landscape. Sometimes the garden represents a journey that follows the course of a

right: Sensitivity in choosing and grouping rocks is vital, whether you are working in symbolism or creating a distillation of a landscape.

Ignore the *brilliance*

Of your intellect

And *return* to the

Unconscious vastness

Of *unknowing*

gushing stream from its origins high in the mountains until it broadens to a quietly flowing river and continues through more gentle scenery until it reaches the sea or opens out into a still lake, perhaps dotted with islands. The landscape provides a focus for meditation: the viewer "sees" the water moving, "hears" the sounds of the wind and waves, and "smells" the salt air. This practice of "entering" the landscape calms the mind as worldly cares are set aside, and the limited space of the garden can appear to expand immeasurably.

In the dry landscape where the sanzon *with its central water-falling stone is used to depict a cascade, the basic configuration may be extended to include other rock groupings that set the scene. The vertical face of the water-falling stone is striated and could even have a notch at the top, suggesting years of erosion. A stone slab bridge set across the front of the "waterfall" further strengthens the illusion and adds depth to the scene.*

Dry Garden Design

A turbulent mountain torrent might be depicted with light-colored rounded cobbles, while farther down, the scale may be reduced to fine grit to suggest gently flowing water. Another way of looking at cascades in dry gardens is to imagine that the water table has dropped temporarily and that the stream will soon be running again.

THE ILLUSION OF WATER

One of the main ways that the flow and movement of water is suggested in the dry garden is by raking the grit or gravel into patterns. The contouring reflects the flow and calmness of the water. Long straight parallel lines denote still water. Where the surface is punctuated with rocks or island groupings, ripples and eddies are suggested by raking around the shapes. Strong currents and choppy seas are represented by more dramatic wave patterns and spirals. The image of a lake or sea can be strengthened by a boat-shaped rock.

In a small courtyard garden, a stream could be depicted as running diagonally across the scene, perhaps filling a small pool along its route. The stream could be suggested with small flat stones or slate shards laid so they overlap one another to denote flow and movement in a particular direction. Alternatively, a combination of cobblestones, pebbles, and larger rocks would give a more naturalistic representation. Cross the imaginary stream with a simple bridge or stepping-stones. The pool could be dug out slightly so the stream appears to drop down into it, but the water

"surface" must be absolutely flat and level, and covered with coarse sand or very fine gravel if the illusion is to work.

Minimalist dry gardens do contain plants, and when clipped into shapes, they can take on the form and character of rock. Moss is often used to strengthen a rock grouping set within gravel, symbolizing vegetation growing on an island, perhaps. The greenery is usually confined to a narrow area around the base of the rock, and further spread into the gravel is controlled. In hot, dry conditions, creeping plants like thyme and other alpine carpeters may be used.

A rocky "crag" may support the growth of a single stunted, weather-beaten tree, perhaps depicted by a skillfully trained pine. It is important to keep the planting in scale with the rocks. Put the rock skeleton in place before the plants, and prune trees and shrubs to size, or remove altogether if the composition becomes unbalanced. Small-leaved evergreens are less visually distracting and can create backdrops for rock configurations such as the *sanzon*. Sedges could denote marshy ground next to a pool. Plants should be muted and largely green so as not to upset the tranquil scene.

left: Strengthening the illusion that water is present, a simple arcing stone bridge crosses a pebble stream that feeds into a gravel pool.
above right: Carefully laid dark-colored flat pebbles represent the flow of water. Pale cobbles and gravel make a stream bank.

Symbolic Water

Water has deep symbolic meaning to the Japanese, perhaps because the country is composed of many separate islands surrounded by sea. The mountainous landscape provides very high annual rainfall. With the ever-present danger of earthquakes and *tsunami* (tidal waves), the people living on the narrow coastal plains have a healthy respect for water, but of course they also recognize its life-giving qualities.

In the Zen garden, water is of such importance that even in the *kare-san-sui* (dry garden) maintaining the illusion of its presence is of paramount importance. A stylized watercourse running through the garden may be viewed as our journey through life, beginning with youthful springs, waterfalls, and cascades, moving to the rivers of middle age, and finally to the ocean of wisdom, understanding, and oneness with the universe.

THE MUTABLE ELEMENT

Water is a yin element with strange qualities and moods. Fast-moving water generates *ki* energizing the space around it. The negative ions released by waterfalls or waves are known to be of benefit to our health. In a cascade lit by sunlight, each droplet sparkles like crystal, and the sight and sound of the moving water is at once soothing and uplifting. But in a shady pool, water can appear dark, perhaps a little ominous, and full of mystery.

Water is mutable, taking the shape of any container into which it is poured. This is symbolic of what Zen teaches about being open, not rigid in our thinking. Water challenges our perception of reality and is paradoxical in nature. In winter water will sometimes change its character completely to become ice. But ice and water are merely different states of the same element, just as life and death are both natural states of our human existence. You can occasionally see the bottom of a pool, but at other times the surface acts like a mirror and the water appears solid. Reflected objects look as though they are in the water, but of course this is just an illusion.

It is water's ability to produce either a true or distorted image that explains its tremendous

above: *A reflecting bowl captures an image of bamboo. When mind is free of thoughts and emotions, it too reflects an undistorted image.*

left: A beautifully constructed naturalistic water feature with cascades tumbling into a pool.

symbolic significance in Zen. Water represents mind. When mind becomes pure and clear and is not contaminated by thoughts and emotions, it reflects a perfect image of everything around it. In other words, it sees the world, the true nature of things, without distortion. The relationship between mind and reality is often described symbolically in haiku poems about water and the moon. This is why clean, clear water is desirable in the Zen garden and why muddy or stagnant water is to be avoided.

Enlightenment is like

The reflection of the moon

in water

The *moon* does not get wet

The water is not *separated*

When we contemplate the surface of a pool, watching how ripples and refractions appear with the slightest disturbance, it is easy to see the relationship between the state of pure mind and mind disturbed by thoughts and emotions. No sooner have you stilled the mind when a thought enters your head and disturbs the tranquility that you have achieved. Fortunately, you can learn to prolong these periods of serenity by practicing mindfulness and meditation.

35

From ancient times, worshipers visiting Shinto shrines were required to cleanse their hands and mouths with water in a purification ritual. Springs and waterfalls were worshiped alongside other natural features. This ritual was absorbed into the Zen tea ceremony, where participants cleanse mind and spirit at the tsukubai.

Water Garden Origins

Between the eighth and eleventh centuries, the Japanese aristocracy built large water gardens, absorbing elements of Taoist mythology into their design. In one account of paradise, five floating mystical isles supported by fifteen giant turtles were inhabited by birds and beasts of purest white, and immortals flew around on the backs of cranes. Today, peculiarly shaped crane and turtle islands are still created in lakes and lotus pools in Japan. The Chinese Jodo or Pure Land sect of Buddhism was also influential. Their view of paradise was similar: immortal beings, serenaded by heavenly music, floated in boats that moved through a landscape filled with flowers. Paintings of this world were given to followers so they would know what pleasures awaited them, and it was not long before the Paradise Garden, with its large lotus pools, emerged as a style. The lotus flower is the Buddhist symbol of enlightenment (*satori*): the plant's roots are buried deep in the stinking mud of human passions, but it grows up through the water and flowers under the sky, symbolizing the mind opening up to revelation.

Centuries ago, certain guidelines emerged concerning the design of natural water features. One states that water should always flow in a natural fashion, which would seem to preclude the use of fountains.

Waterfalls were classified by the number of cascades they contained—the simplest is the curtain fall, where the water-falling stone is wide and level and flanked by two slightly taller stones or *wakiishi*, which help to direct the flow. The most complicated is the uneven fall, where water tumbles down from many different points. Between these extremes are the narrow single fall and the two- and three-step broken falls. Water should flow into an uncluttered pool, and the cascade may be balanced by a bridge crossing directly in front. Legend says that the Japanese Buddhist deity Acala let it be known that any waterfall measuring three feet (one meter) high was a representation of his body, and this is one reason why waterfalls are such a common feature of Zen gardens.

POOL DESIGN

The traditional gourd-shaped pond is roughly a figure-eight in outline, and the *kokoro* (enlightened heart pool) is actually shaped like an inverted heart. The apex of both these shapes (the point farthest

away from the viewer) is emphasized by a small tree and rock formation. Indeed, all pools should have a similar focal point, such as a stone lantern. With any natural pond shape, the widest section should be nearer the viewer to emphasize perspective. If possible, a pool should be set at the far end of the garden, with sightlines leading up to the waterfall.

All rivers run to the *ocean*

without filling it up

All *water* comes from it

without ever emptying it

Try to avoid revealing the pool all at once. The water should really be glimpsed though deliberate openings in the planting, and the waterfall in particular should come as a surprise to the viewer. Whether they are substantial features of larger pools or merely symbolic representations in smaller ponds, islands help to create these changing views. They should never be set in the middle of the water because this usually looks unnatural. Planting of the island can also be used to create an illusion of distance, with larger and smaller trees and shrubs carefully positioned to manipulate our perception of space.

No one looks
for their *reflection* in
running waters

Water in Your Garden

The greens of the garden always seem fresher after rain or first thing in the morning when covered with a heavy dew. Rocks and stepping stones develop a beautiful luster when wet, droplets of water sparkle on leaf and flower, and the greens seem somehow deeper and richer. In Japan, gardens are sometimes sprinkled with water to mimic a recent shower before the arrival of guests, especially along the *roji* (dewy path) prior to the tea ceremony. This is a practice you could copy when you have visitors and the garden is looking a little dry and dusty.

Even if you can only hear its sound, the presence of water exerts a profound psychological influence. It calms us when we are feeling agitated, and during the hot summer months it cools and refreshes us. The sight of a waterfall is frequently uplifting, reminding us of the way the spirit is constantly renewed. Reflections can cause our mood to deepen and become more contemplative, and the images created on the water's surface add immensely to our enjoyment of the garden, the colors and forms being magically enhanced. During the day you can follow the progress of clouds across the sky, and at night the moon and stars are captured in the water.

below: *A modern glass sculpture like a sheet of melting glacial ice makes an intriguing fountain set among the pebbles.*

To maintain the reflective potential of the pool, make sure much of the surface is clear, and is not completely covered with the foliage of plants like water lilies. Of course, you do not actually need a pool to produce reflections. Ceramic bowls of water of different sizes set at varying heights will bring the sky into the garden.

The sound of running water can vary from a soft trickle to a loud gushing, depending on the kind of feature. In the garden in general and particularly in small courtyards where surrounding walls may amplify the sound, you need to take care that a water feature does not impinge too much on the

above: A constant trickle of water coming from a bamboo pipe feeds a small mossy pool. The sound is wonderfully soothing.

serene atmosphere of your Zen garden. With a waterfall or wall-mounted water spout, the force of water hitting the surface can be lessened by placing a stone or pebble to break the cascade's fall. This can also make the cascade quieter and make it sound less hollow and more natural.

CRYSTAL CLEAR WATER

The apparent clarity of water in a stream or pool reduces with depth. It is good to include some shallow features to emphasize the purity of the water; the image is enhanced when the floor of a pool or stream is covered in gravel, cobblestones, or pebbles. Fish are wonderfully relaxing to watch as they glide through the shallows, but in deep water they have a habit of disappearing. A relatively shallow pool that shelves gently to a deeper area is ideal, but the fish will need a place to hide from predators and an area at least three feet (one meter) in depth in which to lie low during cold periods when the surface may be frozen. The larger the fish, the deeper the water needed, so check with your supplier before introducing fish. Koi carp will become quite tame with regular feeding and are traditionally associated with Japanese gardens, but they are notorious for eating pond plants, and you may prefer to introduce a less destructive kind.

Although Zen emphasizes naturalness, stylized water features can be used to create an abstract image in the same way that rock in the dry garden can be nonrepresentational. The properties and qualities of water mean that it combines easily with many different media, including natural stone, ceramic, terracotta, metal, wood, and glass. And the inclusion of rectangular pools or simple, man-made water features will bring life to stark, minimalist garden designs.

Woodland Gardens

Woodland gardens are rare in Japan, but there is precedence for creating features in woodland. Shinto shrines are found in the mountains in shady clearings surrounded by trees, and the Zen tea house is designed to give the impression of a rude hermit's retreat hidden deep in the forest.

A stand of mature trees has the effect of dampening sounds coming from outside, and in woodland there is a particular quality of hushed stillness. The overhead canopy creates enclosure and restricts the amount of sky visible. This tends to focus the eye down, and the surrounding vegetation appears closer, making it easier for us to bring our awareness within. In spring and summer, the light filtering through the overhead foliage is green and consequently very soothing, and apart from a burst of color in spring and fall, deciduous woodland is visually quiet and serene.

DESIGNING AROUND TREES

If you have an area of woodland in your garden, a row of trees, or even a single mature specimen, you can create a naturalistic Zen garden in the shade below. First, take a look at the amount of light coming in. Dappled shade with pools of sunlight is ideal because there is a good balance between yang light and yin shade. If you have a dense overhead network of branches, very little light will filter through and the space will tend to feel gloomy and oppressive. A qualified tree surgeon can advise you, even recommending the removal of entire trees. This sound rather drastic, but most trees planted by man need to be managed. Unmaintained woodland can become a tangled mass of saplings, fallen trees,

and dense undergrowth. Keeping the mature trees, felling those that present a danger, and clearing the space in between will transform the site. Extra light reaching the woodland floor will trigger of a flush of new growth—in Eastern terms, *ki* (energy) will flow freely once more.

When you introduce new planting, use a very restricted palette to maintain a tranquil atmosphere. On acid soil, resist the temptation to fill the space with gaudy rhododendron and azalea cultivars. A scheme of white, cream, and touches of yellow, with blues and mauves coming in at various times of year, mirrors the colors of natural woodland. Plant drifts of woodland bulbs and spring-flowering herbs and, to bridge the space between canopy and ground, introduce shrub groupings and one or two elegant woodland trees. On acid soil, blue and soft purple hydrangeas will color well, and there is a wealth of Japanese and Chinese evergreens to choose from.

A stream crossed by a simple log bridge would add to the scene, but the pump must be adequately filtered. Rock formations among the trees suggest a mountain forest; if possible, use porous stone, which will be rapidly colonized by mosses and algae in shade. This will help make new woodland planting feel more established. Pathways should seem like natural forest trails. On a totally flat site, organic contouring will create depth and add interesting design possibilities.

right: Woodland gardens often have a feeling of stillness and tranquility. Soild rock helps to generate such an atmosphere.

Moss Gardens

Moss gardens can be the most tranquil of spaces. If you have ever experienced what it is like to be in the midst of a great old forest high up in clear, moist mountain air, with streams crisscrossing the ground, and tresses of moss hanging from the branches, you will know the magical feel that a shady moss garden can engender.

An area given over to moss needs little in the way of adornment. You can create a beautiful scene by adding just a few glossy evergreen shrubs; perhaps one or two small, elegant trees; some ferns for lightness; rocks and cobblestones for the moss to infiltrate, and a slowly meandering stepping-stone path. This is just the kind of wild garden that can be found leading to a traditional Zen tea house, when it is know as the *roji* (dewy path). Progress through the garden prepares the visitor both mentally and spiritually for the ceremony to come.

CULTIVATING A CARPET

Moss will colonize any damp, shady place where the soil is left undisturbed. You will find it growing on porous rocks that can absorb moisture, like limestone and sandstone; on pieces of wood; on damp walls; and, in areas with very clean air and a moist atmosphere, on the trunks of trees. In Western gardens, moss is often viewed as a weed, and the different species are all lumped in under the same heading.

In Japan, because of the very high rainfall, moss grows very easily and is deliberately cultivated. Gardeners are able to identify the different kinds, and they are merged together to create a subtle tapestry in myriad shades of green. Moss carpets

above: *Moss gardens grow best in shade, and the widest diversity of species is found where the ground has been undisturbed for years.*

are used in place of lawns in suitably shaded areas, such as gardens encircled by buildings or mature trees. They look particularly attractive surrounding shady pools, contrast well with rock and gravel, and make useful groundcover under evergreen shrubs.

As they are primitive plants, mosses are easily scorched by fertilizer. They grow well on peaty soils and ones rich in well-rotted organic matter, such as leaf mold, but the main requirement is moisture. If you want algae, mosses, and lichens to colonize your concrete paving, add a little peat to the mixture and spray with sequestered iron solution.

Moss may suffer on very free-draining soils and in hot dry conditions, and in low rainfall areas it

alternative is to weed by hand when the seedlings are very small and have not developed much of a root system. When working in a moss area or planting a new shrub, try to disturb the soil as little as possible because this brings a new set of weed seeds to the surface and, given enough light, they will quickly germinate. Over time, weeds stop coming through, and a stable moss carpet can be established which needs very little care.

may be necessary to water regularly, even in shady conditions. Happily the plants often recover even when they have turned brown, but it may take a while. One of the biggest problems in establishing a moss garden is controlling the growth of shade-tolerant weeds and grasses. Weedkillers can be used, but they rather go against the Zen philosophy of not damaging the environment. The best

If you find it hard to establish moss, a similar look can be created with baby's tears or mind-your-own-business (*Soleirolia soleirolii*). It is normally sold as a houseplant, and in a pot it creates a dome of tiny leaves, but when grown outdoors it spreads to form a thin film of leaves. Similar in its effect and wonderful for colonizing the gaps in shady, rough stone paths is creeping mint (*Mentha requienii*).

Tuning in to Nature

If you want to make your garden into a natural haven, send out the message via your thoughts and actions that your garden is truly a sanctuary for all creatures. The world is a living system in which all the elements are interconnected, and although we are just one part of this complex web, we have a huge impact on it. Zen teaches respect for every living thing, but in the garden it is sometimes hard not to differentiate between good and bad. We ask "is it a weed or a flower?" Insects are often referred to as the gardener's friend or foe. You can only act in a way that feels right for you, but remember that everything has its place in the scheme of things and killing one group of pests, however lowly or undesirable, is bound to have an effect along the line. Ultimately we are harming ourselves.

Animals are very sensitive to atmosphere. A good wildlife garden is a peaceful place where humans go quietly and move carefully, minimizing their impact on the surroundings, mindful of the consequences of their actions. Animals and birds will soon become accustomed to you sharing their home, and if you are very privileged, they may eventually become fairly tame. Position your seating and paths carefully so as not to intrude unnecessarily on their habitat. Animals will get used to seeing you moving to and fro and feel safe and

above: A small stream running through a wildflower meadow creates many different habitats for birds, insects, and other animals.
right: Newly emerged from its pupal case, a dragonfly recovers its strength before flying off. These jewellike insects are attracted by water.

unthreatened if you stick to prescribed routes and develop something of a routine. Learn to stand or sit very quietly; remain absolutely motionless and observe in minute detail the everyday comings and goings of wildlife. Your understanding of the natural world will deepen, as will your appreciation of its marvelous complexity. After only fifteen minutes sitting and watching at the edge of a pond you may start to feel calm, relaxed, and peaceful.

A bird *sang*

Everyone listened

The *sermon* is preached

Said the *master*

DEVELOPING YOUR SENSES

Gardens that teem with bird and insect life are not just a feature of the countryside: you can find them in the heart of the urban landscape in towns and cities everywhere. Nature will always find a way to reclaim lost ground—think of the way tree seedlings colonize brick walls, and wild plants push up through cracks in the concrete. And if we give her a helping hand, and create an environment in which insects, birds, and other animals can thrive, then life really begins to burgeon. In these green oases, nature can be so abundant that, if you close your eyes and just listen, you can imagine yourself sitting on a riverbank or standing in the middle of woodland on a warm spring day.

Once in a while, it is a good exercise to close your eyes and simply concentrate on what you

can hear. The more closely you listen, the more aware you will become of the multitudinous layerings of sound: liquid warbles, chatterings, and chirrupings all mixed up with the flutter of wings, the steady hum of foraging bees, and the zoom of dragonflies. With our busy lives we rarely take time

out to fully experience the evocative sights and sounds of dawn and dusk. In these twilight moments, you can often see bats hunting for moths and other insects, and if you remain absolutely quiet and still, you may just glimpse some shy nocturnal animal going about its business.

I have moved into three new houses which at first had only grass for a backyard. Thankfully, birds arrived the moment I introduced trees. Gradually, more insect life appeared, which provided food for other animals. With plants keeping the ground shaded and moist, frogs, toads, and newts moved in, as did slugs and snails, but pests do little damage if you maintain a balance of wildlife in the garden.

Making a Garden for Wildlife

Some say that a garden is not truly alive without water, and certainly the level of wildlife soars once this element is introduced. My first "pond" was a plastic tub sunk into the ground with a couple of house bricks as a perch for bathing birds. I put in some submerged aquatics, planted around the edge to give extra cover, and waited to see what would happen. Out of the blue, a dragonfly appeared. I have no idea where it came from. It was a hot, dry summer that year, and the birds would regularly line up for a drink; as the temperature soared, the frogs took up residence.

Animals need shelter from the elements and from predators, a source of food and water for themselves and their young, and somewhere to reproduce successfully. You might not be able to achieve all these things in your wildlife garden, but animals will certainly drop by even if it is just to use the garden as a temporary food stop. Here are a few things you can do to encourage wildlife.

- *Plant trees and large shrubs for bird perching and night roosting—berrying varieties are particularly useful.*
- *Maintain bird feeding stations throughout the year, away from potential predators.*

- *Provide fresh water for drinking and bathing. In colder areas, this is vital during the winter months when natural water sources may freeze over. Allow safe access to ponds for all animals.*
- *Put up bird and bat boxes if you have suitable sites.*
- *Plant a wide variety of nectar-rich perennials and flowering shrubs to attract bees, butterflies, moths, and other insects.*
- *Plant species and single-flowered varieties, which are the most attractive to insects. With a high insect population you will attract more birds, bats, and dragonflies to your garden.*
- *Do not be too neat. Create a log pile in a shady corner and leave it undisturbed for fungi, insects, mollusks, small mammals, and amphibians. Leave an area of weeds, wild plants, and long grass for butterflies and other insects to lay their eggs and as a food source for caterpillars. In fall, resist the temptation to cut down dying stems. Allow fruits and seed heads to develop as a natural food source for birds and other animals during*

above: *Spider webs are like works of art, especially when they are sparkling with dewdrops or caught by the frost.*
right: *Frogs will inhabit any damp spot and are useful for keeping down insect pests in the garden. Even a tiny pond will attract them.*

The old *pond*

Frog jumps in—

Splash!

winter and leave perennial foliage where it is. It provides shelter for animals as well as insulating the plants themselves. It is also easier to pull off the dead leaves in spring.

- Cover the ground with plants, especially around ponds, and create a tiered understory beneath trees, mimicking natural woodland.

- Go organic. Stop using chemicals to control weeds, pests, and diseases. Look after your soil by adding plenty of organic matter. Do not dig it—keep adding it to the surface; the worms will do the rest. Healthy plants are more resistant to pests and disease, and a well-fed and mulched soil will go a long way to achieving this.

Courtyard Gardens

You can build a *tsuboniwa* (courtyard garden) in the smallest of spaces. A garden of some kind is possible in seemingly impossible areas—a narrow, windswept urban entranceway, an atrium, or a dark side passage between two building. Just make sure that the drainage is adequate before applying any surfacing on top of concrete, and use one or two carefully chosen plants in containers.

The Zen approach—simplicity in design and attention to detail—is useful in a small garden. An illusion of space can be created by leaving as much as two thirds of the area plain and then creating an esthetically pleasing composition by carefully positioning plants and hard landscaping elements. Try to link features of the building with the ground plan, relating the proportions of both to create a sense of unity. Draw your design out on paper, and try out various alternatives. A minimalist scheme will prevent the space from feeling cluttered. Keep surfaces clean and weedfree at all times.

AN OUTDOOR ROOM

Where high walls surround the plot, you can bring the scale down by painting the walls a pale, neutral color up to ceiling height. If the walls are brick, a smooth rendering will simplify the backdrop. You could also attach wooden or bamboo trellis to the walls. In a courtyard surrounded by tall buildings, cladding that follows a horizontal line takes the emphasis off the height of the walls. Sometimes it is possible to use the same material as a continuation across part of the floor. An example might be horizontal wooden planks mirrored by decking in the same type of wood with a contrast of gravel.

With walls creating a very strong rectilinear feel, there are several design options. One is to stay with the straight lines, emphasizing the simplicity with a straight pathway or area of low decking running along one wall and slightly offset from the doorway. Alternatively, you could introduce a curve such as a line of stepping stones within gravel or mossy planting, to counter the severity of a straight path. Or, you might choose to create a balanced, rather

more static arrangement with two points of interest set diagonally opposite one another—an upright bamboo with a rock grouping as a counterpoint.

A RESTRICTED PALETTE

In a very small space, restrict your color palette, concentrating on introducing a limited amount of textural contrast. If you have a single straight path, make the most of its potential for adding dramatic

below: This beautifully proportioned balcony garden contrasts smooth lines with random shapes. The bougainvillea is vivid against the wall.

interest and create a paving design that really makes you aware of the steps you are taking.

Pale wall colors and flooring materials reflect what light there is and energize gloomy corners. A shady basement garden below street level could have walls painted white with white gravel surfacing and a glossy leaved fatsia in one corner. Black slate stepping stones would make a stylish contrast. With greenery on one side and a mirror on the wall opposite, you could also create the illusion of a doorway leading to another part of the garden, again increasing the sense of spaciouness.

Be *empty*, be still

Watch everything

Just *come* and go

A Room with a View

If only a glass wall separates your garden from your living room, then the garden can be a source of inspiration all through the year and you will be able to experience its changing moods and the subtle ebb and flow of the seasons. When creatively lit, the garden can be admired even at night. In the West, patio doors and conservatories have transformed the way we view our gardens. On warm sunny days we open the doors, and the boundary between indoors and out disappears. Japanese homes have been using such sliding screen walls for centuries, and have refined the art of framing views from the house. The process is rather like the way a photographer focuses in on a particular image, setting up the camera in such a way that unwanted elements are excluded and the subject is viewed from the best possible angle.

Views from the doors and windows of a house can be manipulated in the same way, creating sightlines through to greater and lesser focal points and using screens and planting to block out other

areas to minimize distraction. Indoors, simple roll-down blinds can be used to shield the room from strong sunlight, but can also assist in framing the view; for example, if the roof lines of houses appear above the boundary wall, you can block them out and improve your outlook.

INSIDE AND OUT

The garden presents a layered, three-dimensional image, and although the doors and windows are used to frame this picture initially, other elements within the garden can also be used to direct the eye, such as tree trunks or staggered bamboo columns on either side of a path, or the overhanging arch of a tree or shrub. Remember, objects nearer the viewer will seem larger and therefore block out more of the background.

It is possible to create the illusion of space and feel a greater connection with the world outside the window when indoors and outdoors are linked visually. One way to do this is to build a veranda, arbor, or a decked or paved area that extends from the house. Slightly raised, it gives you a subtly different view of the garden. The traditional use of a

above: Sliding glass panels lead straight to the garden in this Japanese house. The boundary between indoors and out is hardly noticeable.

large slab of stone at the doorway links the two environments both practically and symbolically. Experiment by using the same color scheme and flooring materials indoors and out, and by mirroring the position of key elements like seating and potted plants to further emphasize the link. This technique is particularly useful where space is at a premium.

COMPOSING A PICTURE

Where the outlook to the garden is via a wall of glass, you could bring water right up to the house by building a formal pool flush with the window. Alternatively, introduce the sound of running water indoors by having a moving water feature right next to the opening.

Some outdoor spaces are so small that you cannot actually walk around in them, but even these present opportunity for the Zen gardener to compose a serene picture and a focus for contemplation. Without living material a still-life composition is unlikely to reflect the constant mutability of nature and the passage of time with the changing seasons. A deciduous shrub or small tree planted in a pot provides a solution: use dwarf varieties or bonsai to keep in scale with a truly tiny space. Seasonal cut flowers also last well outdoors and might provide a good alternative where growing conditions are very poor. Just select a single bloom, leaf, or branch. Caring for the arrangement could become part of a daily practice in mindfulness.

Another way to create change would be to use fine gravel as a surfacing material and to rake in different patterns periodically.

part three

Making a Garden

How *transient* is life!

Every minute is to be *grasped*

Time *waits* for nobody

Planning a Water Feature

When planning a water feature, it is vital to have a strong image of the kind of effect you want to create at the outset. If you think you want a rock and water garden like a mountain stream, consider how natural it will look in your garden.

There are a number of factors to consider when choosing the right spot. A sunny, sheltered site which is not overhung by trees will produce the healthiest water environment and, therefore, one most beneficial for fish and wildlife. Ideally, the area should receive direct light for at least half the day. However, a shady pool surrounded by mosses and ferns can be wonderfully evocative. A shady pool can still support a diverse community, as well as less fussy fish, like golden orf, if the pool is big enough, and certainly if the water is circulated by a pump. Overhanging trees can be a problem, especially deciduous ones that fill the water with leaves in fall. Debris can not only block the pump, but also if not removed, it sinks to the bottom, where there is less oxygen and rots, producing noxious byproducts. Removing this sludge is a smelly business! You can net the pond, but this is unsightly and can be dangerous for birds and other wildlife. Take care not to allow poisonous leaves like laburnum to drop into the water.

REFLECTIONS

One of the most important considerations for the Zen gardener, for whom water is such a symbolic element, is reflection. A sheltered pool receiving light will produce clear reflections of surrounding plants, trees, and sculptural features. Fountains, water jets, and cascades disturb the surface,

above: *It is relatively easy to make the single waterfall look convincing as part of a natural water feature.*

For a natural water feature your choice of pump is dictated by the desired flow rate (number of gallons or liters per hour), the height to which the water is to be pumped, and the distance traveled. A good water-garden supplier will be able to help you with the necessary calculations. To estimate the flow rate, build the cascade with the rocks roughly in position, and then fill two-gallon buckets with water and ask someone to pour them down the slope at different rates. You should be able to judge by eye what flow rate looks right for the feature, and then convert buckets-per-minute to gallons-per-hour. Powerful pumps are more expensive, but it is better to buy a model with some power to spare rather than one that is just

distorting the images, so consider carefully what kind of effect you want before installing a pump. For the best reflections, site the pool so the sun is behind you when you are looking from the main vantage point. Otherwise, with the sun shining into your eyes, you could also suffer the problem of glare from the water surface.

MOVING WATER

A sloping site is ideal for creating a naturalistic pool with a water cascade. It is much harder to create a convincing effect on a flat site, although the soil dug out of the hole for the pond can be used to contour the ground and create the necessary gradient. When introducing moving water, you also need a convenient electricity supply. It may be impractical to run the cable over a long distance, especially in an established garden, where it may be difficult to bury it underground.

left: *These cascades were built on a gently sloping site. The stone wall effectively dams the water, creating a shallow pool.*

above: *You can make more of water flowing over steps in a shallow gradient by creating multiple cascades.*

right, because the flow can be increased if conditions change over time. Submersible pumps are the easiest to install, but you can also buy surface pumps that require separate waterproof housing. If it is carefully planned, the addition of a water feature will transform your garden.

Building a Natural Pond

When making a pond, the first task is to excavate the hole. Do this by hand or use a bulldozer for larger projects. If you plan to reuse the soil for planting, keep topsoil separate from the subsoil, which is poisonous to plants. Mark out the shape of the pool and make a note of where the deepest point will be and how the sides are to be contoured; for example, you may want shelves on which to place planting baskets. A gently sloping shallow area provides safe access for wildlife. Avoid

steep sides, except at the point where a waterfall enters the pool. The critical factor is making sure the top edges of the pool are absolutely level—the tiniest discrepancy multiplies alarmingly, and no amount of marginal planting will cover up the mistake. Check the level by spanning the pool with a plank of wood with a carpenter's level on top.

above: A cobblestone bank shelves gently into an informal lily pond whose margins are densely planted with lush moisture lovers.

LINING THE POOL

A rigid, preformed liner is an option for your pool, but the hole has to be dug fairly accurately to accommodate it and you are limited to a few shapes. Avoid colored liners: they usually look unnatural and produce a poor reflection. The easiest and most effective way to make a pool waterproof is to line it with good-quality black butyl rubber. Again, seek advice on how to calculate the dimensions of the sheet, allowing plenty of spare material to work with.

Heavy-duty butyl is pretty tough, but it is best to lay it on a thick bed of soft sand and then a sheet of commercial underlay. The weight of water may just force a sharp stone through, causing a leak. Firm the sides and base of the pond, compacting the soil to prevent movement, then apply the sand, firming it and smoothing it with your hands or using a wooden or plastic plasterer's trowel. Carefully fit the underlay in place. If possible, choose a sunny day to work, and lay the liner out on a flat surface for a few hours because the heat helps to make the butyl more pliable and easier to handle. Enlist some help to lift the sheet and lay it in position, then gradually work the material into the contours of the pond, tucking and folding into the corners.

Do not trim off the excess at this stage, but fill the pool with water. The weight may well pull the liner farther down. Leave for several hours before trimming the edges. You could extend the butyl into a shallow depression filled with soil to create a bog garden. Trim off excess liner with a sharp cutting tool; then hold the edges in place by tucking them underneath the soil or beneath cemented-in rocks. Camouflage the pool edge with pieces of stone or spreading plant material, making sure there is a good overhang to avoid seeing the liner.

MAKING A CASCADE

If a stream or set of cascades runs into the pond, prepare the ground with sand and underlay as for a pool and lay a strip of butyl along the water course. Allow a sizable overlap into the pond to lessen the risk of leaks at the seam. Disguise the channel with overhanging plants or, if the cascade is fairly wide, with flat pieces of stone, cobblestones, and gravel. On a slope, hold these in place with cement. Mini waterfalls look most realistic running over large pieces of stone, but the liner must be protected by a soft bed of folded butyl and underlay to prevent puncture. Run the electric cable through buried armored ducting and connect it to a circuit breaker. Camouflage the point at which the pump cable enters the pool, and hide the water pipe that carries water back up to the header pool at the top of the cascade.

Naturalistic water features can look out of place with certain styles of garden, particularly adjacent to modern minimalist architecture. But you can make pools and watercourses to any shape—a narrow stone-edged rill might feed a circular pool, for example, or you could create a series of interlocking rectangular pools at different levels with simple overflows.

Formal Pools and Other Features

When using butyl liner, use the techniques outlined on page 57, but in pools with near-vertical sides, the liner must carefully folded and pleated at the corners. Such pools are not as nature friendly as wildlife pools, although a sloping entry point or ledge for marginal planting will help by allowing small animals access to the pond. For larger, more complex constructions, it is always advisable to hire a contractor, especially when building with concrete which requires wooden shuttering. To increase the reflective quality of the water, coat concrete pools with black sealant.

above: Square stepping stones seem to float on the water in this modern Zen-styled lily pool. An atmosphere of tranquility prevails.

There are several different options for edging pools, depending on the look you want. Lengths of heavy wood will produce a more natural feel for a rectangular pool than dressed stone. Reclaimed railroad ties are also useful for building a raised pool. Vertical log sections give a more informal look, suitable for edging wildlife ponds. Place carefully to avoid piercing the liner. An overhanging deck hides the liner and works well with most pool styles.

A gently shelving beach of cobblestones that gradually disappears under water creates a wonderfully simple pool for contemplation. Excavate an undulating shape, creating a gently shelving depression; line it with butyl and then cover with stones. Extend the beach out at the viewing side of the pool and surround the shoreline elsewhere with dense water-margin planting.

TRADITIONAL TSUKUBAI

Sink a waterproof container into the ground and cover with a sheet of rigid wire mesh to support the cobblestones. Fit a submersible pump; feed the electric cable through armored ducting, and set a piece of plastic tubing over the outlet ready for the pump to be switched on. A piece of bamboo forms the water spout. Fill the tank, then tilt the stone basin so the water pours cleanly into the reservoir.

SAFE WATER FEATURES

If you want the sound of running water, but have small children or no room for a pond, build a feature where the water reservoir is underground. There are a number of variations to the basic *tsukubai* (illustrated above right), including the Japanese *chozubachi*, a tall drinking water jar, which is sited by a doorway to welcome and refresh guests. In the wall fountain arrangement, water is pumped up from a water tank set below ground. Alternatively, above ground use a wooden half barrel. Hiding the water feed pipe can be tricky

with wall fountains. Ideally, drill through the wall and feed the pipe through, up the back and out again through a decorative spout. If that is not possible, chip out a channel for the pipe and re-cover with mortar or alternatively camouflage it with strategically placed plants.

A more naturalistic feature is the cobbled spring. Sink a reservoir below ground, this time in the center of a shallow depression. Cover with a mesh and then with cobblestones. Extend the stones into the surrounding area. Install a special attachment that produces the effect of a gushing spring.

There is something quite magical about crossing over water or standing on a bridge and watching it flow beneath your feet. Bridges have symbolic meaning in many cultures, and just as passing through a gateway can transport you physically and mentally to another realm, so bridges can make us aware of journeying to a special place within the garden.

Stepping Stones and Bridges

When carefully positioned, a bridge or row of stepping stones will lead the eye across to a particular feature, linking two different areas and helping to strengthen the sense of perspective. Simple bridges, especially those of a graceful arcing design, generate a feeling of balance and stability. In our minds, the connection between bridge and water is so strong that the presence of a bridge can complete the illusion of water in the symbolic dry garden landscape (see also pages 32–33). Stepping stones, which normally represent the yang force of immovability and endurance, can have a surreal quality when they almost appear to float on the surface of a deep, black reflecting pool.

SYMBOLIC CROSSINGS

When the pathway is straight and direct, it tends to dictate swift crossing, but when it meanders, the pace slows right down and we are encouraged to linger along the route, stopping at each twist and turn. We become aware of every footstep and stepping stones remind us that there is just a chance that we might get our feet wet or even fall in if we are not mindful. This slow progress gives us the opportunity to just be. We can enjoy the sights and sounds as we "glide" across the water—watch fish swimming lazily beneath the surface, soak up the reflections, wonder at the disturbances, and listen to the hum of nature all around. It reminds us that on our journey through life we should live each moment in the now and not simply focus on some unseen destination.

A single-span bridge across a narrow channel is not hard to construct. All you need is a large, flat slab of stone, or two or three heavy planks of wood laid side by side, making a walkway wide enough for one person to cross in comfort. Another easy bridge design consists of two parallel posts with a walkway of planks nailed on top.

Whatever the design, it should be immediately obvious that the bridge is solidly constructed; otherwise, it will generate a feeling of unease even before attempts are made to cross. Embed the supports firmly in the ground or set the span on four substantial stones, one at each corner, that are partly buried in the ground for stability.

BRIDGE DESIGN

If your Zen garden has an Eastern feel, try a staggered bridge, where two pieces are touching but slightly offset, the join supported by a central column. There is also the double-span bridge where two virtually identical pieces are placed in line, supported by a heavy stone in midstream. Set your stone on extra pieces of butyl and underlay to cushion the weight. For crossing deeper water, a foundation raft of concrete needs to be laid on

Careful as if crossing a

frozen *river*

Alert as if aware of danger

cushioning underlay to support solid brick piers. In a naturally occurring pool you can also drive wooden posts deep into the bed and build wooden structures from this foundation, but make sure the wood preservative used is not harmful to wildlife.

It is now possible to buy a ready-made plain Japanese-style wooden bridge, and the sculptural form of a simple arc works beautifully in the Zen garden. For a traditional look, you might also try building a zigzag bridge from wooden planks or narrow rectangular stone slabs. When combined with stepping stones, it makes an informal crossing.

above left: *"Floating" stepping stones like these have to be supported on solid pillars if they are to be used.*

right: *This simple arcing stone bridge is both esthetically pleasing and functional. It balances the gnarled pine perfectly.*

Selecting and Placing Rock

In Zen philosophy, real stone is considered almost a living material. It may not be easy to source quarried stone, and it may be expensive to transport stone over any distance, but the genuine article is worth tracking down if you wish to create a dry garden landscape with any resonance.

Local stone is often the best choice because it will not look out of place in your garden. In Japan, granite and granite grit is most commonly used, and it will give you an authentic feel. Its hardness is legendary, and yet with exposure to the elements it weathers to a beautiful patina. Granite stone lanterns and water basins are costly, and pieces made from reconstituted stone can be substituted.

Whatever stone you select, make sure it is not too pale or brightly colored—avoid red or orange tones. Rocks with prominent colored veining or marbling will also be distracting, though subtle striations may give them a certain vitality. Stone that absorbs moisture will tend to weather more rapidly and hence look old and established more quickly. In shade, for example, sandstone often acquires an atmospheric covering of moss.

Groups of five and seven rocks can be built up gradually, starting with the largest and finishing with the smallest to give a broadly triangular outline. The smaller outer rocks serve to lead the eye in to the composition and are often quite deeply buried to give the required profile. Try to match the energy flow of the rocks in each composition by aligning the strata in the same direction. Make sure that individual groupings work well with each other. The rocks provide the structure of the garden, and once they are in place, planting and surfacing can begin.

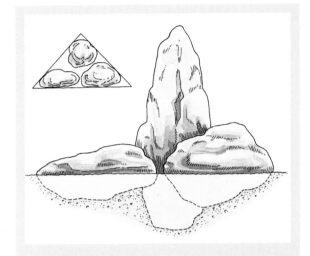

THE *SANZON* ARRANGEMENT

When you are putting the rocks in position, begin with the main stone in the group—for the sanzon arrangement, this would be the tall, upright water-falling stone. Dig a hole large enough to accommodate it and lower it in. Once it appears balanced, compact the soil in around it or ram in rubble. If a large piece still does not feel stable, concrete it in and wait for the mixture to harden properly before attempting to place the other elements. Then add the next main rock and the next, balancing the pieces to create a harmonious picture from all sides. The sanzon has a triangular profile when viewed from above. Traditional Zen gardens also use single rocks and paired rocks that balance one another.

right: *The strong presence of these rocks adds the quality of endurance to the garden. They contrast dramatically with the flowing gravel.*

The gravel used in dry gardens in Japan is a kind of grit or sand. A coarser material might not show the raked patterns so clearly, but in an exposed site or after a spate of bad weather, the lines disappear quite quickly, necessitating reraking. Since raking is a kind of moving meditation, this should not deter the Zen gardener. It is important not to get too attached to the patterns you create!

Surfacing and Planting the Dry Garden

There are several chemical-free ways to combat weeds in gravel. First, avoid notorious self-seeders like lady's mantle (*Alchemilla mollis*) next to gravel areas. You can apply grit or gravel to suitably compacted and leveled rubble, but any weed seeds that drop onto the gravel may germinate and find moisture in the layer beneath. Laying a barrier under the gravel is the best option. A cheap alternative is heavy-grade plastic sheeting, perforated at intervals, especially in depressions, where water is liable to pool. Somewhat more expensive is a permeable membrane that lets rain and air through to the soil, but prevents, or at least controls, weed growth. By cutting cross-shaped openings through the membrane, you can plant directly through and then replace the gravel. The membrane helps conserve moisture below the surface and encourages plant establishment. Obviously, this material has to be fitted around the rock groupings or landscape features created with rock. Another option is to spread a thin layer of concrete beneath the gravel, sealing away the soil for good. This method undoubtedly will control the weeds, but it is not ideal because you have to be very careful to avoid potential planting areas.

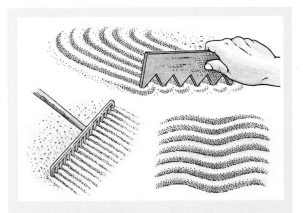

RAKING GRAVEL

Traditionally, a long-handled wooden rake with widely spaced tines is used to rake patterns into coarse grit or fine gravel. This should be laid deep enough to achieve the desired effect—light patterns and a fairly flat finish or deep contours. If the gravel is too coarse, it will be difficult to sculpt. For small areas, a hand-held "comb" can be made by cutting triangular teeth in a piece of wood as shown. Whatever you use, keep the patterns simple and plan your route so you do not have to walk over parts already raked.

Apart from water, the obvious alternative foil for rock, you could also use mown grass or creeping evergreen groundcover. The look is softer and perhaps less surreal, and can be combined with other surfacing materials such as cobblestones (representing a stream through the garden perhaps) as well as selected trees and shrubs. This would also make a tranquil backdrop for a pool.

If we can *just* forget ourselves
We can become one
With our *environment*

Within the highly stylized environs of the dry garden, keep planting to a minimum and confine your selection to plain, small-leaved evergreen shrubs, small specimen trees, and non-flowering groundcover plants. This is only a distillation of nature—one tree could represent a woodland— and planting must be kept in scale with the rock landscape. Improve the soil in planting pockets, using well-rotted organic matter, before applying any kind of mulch or membrane.

The soil in pockets around rocks situated in full sun may get very hot and dry because the stones act like storage heaters. Plants may need to be drought tolerant to survive, and watering while they get established is vital.

left: *The tassellike flower heads of* Miscanthus *(Japanese silver grass) shimmer in the light. Grasses and gravel are natural partners.*

Stepping Stones and Pathways

In the Zen garden, stepping stones are often symbolic of the Way—the spiritual journey through life. When well laid out, they can manipulate the pace at which we walk and cause us to pause at points of interest through the garden. Just like good storytelling, the whole picture unfolds little by little.

Unlike solid pathways, stepping stones emphasize informality. Their layout is so important to Japanese designers they give different configurations names, for example, *chidori* refers to a zigzag pattern, *ganko* (wild geese) to an arcing line.

Even ordinary square concrete paving slabs can be laid in an interesting and dynamic way, creating a sense of movement. Lay the slabs out, creating gentle curves, and check that they are spaced at a comfortable distance to walk on. Consider rotating a slab to create a diamond every so often just for contrast.

CHIDORI

Lay stepping stones firmly, partly burying them for stability. In grass they must be flush with the lawn but in gravel or soil they are traditionally slightly raised for emphasis. Four-way crossroads are always avoided. When working with randomly shaped stones, use smaller pieces to create interesting groupings with larger stones, particularly where the path

GANKO

changes direction. By surrounding parts of a pathway with tall planting or screens, you can create dramatic tension for the visitor before revealing another vista a little way along.

Path intersections feel more comfortable and balanced with a larger, weightier stone, a *garanseki* (foundation stone), at the center. This encourages you to stop and consider in a relaxed manner which way to go. Traditionally, a *katsunugi-ishi* (the shoe-removing stone), a very large flat stone, is placed at the entrance to the house or veranda, and this also strengthens the visual link between the house and the garden—inside and out.

PATH INTERSECTION

If you cannot get suitable natural stone slabs, consider creating your own with cement. Excavate the shapes you require to a depth of at least 3 inches (75 mm), more for large stones, to prevent cracking. Give the cement something to lock on to by using pieces of chicken wire, cut to shape and pinned down, or moisten the soil and tamp in a quantity of limestone chips. Mix a 4:1 or 5:1 ratio of local sand to cement. Add water to achieve a fairly firm consistency and fill in the mold. Create texture by working gravel or stones into the surface. Before it dries completely, scrape with a trowel and brush with a stiff, dampened nylon-bristle brush to create a rough, natural-looking surface.

When paved pathways are associated with buildings, they can be laid in a straight line. A

above: *Texture is all important in the design of a pathway. Here large random cobblestones are bounded by dressed stone.*

textured and somewhat uneven surface will increase awareness of each step taken. In an informal area you can create paths from random stone and large flat cobblestones with spaces for soil and mossy planting between. For a more structured pattern, try combining man-made paving or dressed stone with cobblestones and pebbles, or use tiles or slates set on edge to create a design.

Edge gravel paths with stone, concrete blocks, path-edging strips, pressure-treated gravel boards, or log-roll pinned in position with wooden stakes. In a woodland or wild garden, consider bark chip, shards of slate, gravel, or flat beach pebbles laid with or without an edging. Compacted earth would also suffice, with a few pieces of stone across muddy spots. A narrow winding path built for one is fine in a wild garden, but a path serving a main entranceway, particularly in a more formal setting, should create a sense of space.

Decks and Boardwalks

Wood is a wonderful surfacing material that looks totally natural in the garden. It combines easily with stone and gravel, and is an excellent foil for foliage. Cut lumber also makes a useful bridging material between house and garden. Because of its insulating properties, wood feels good to sit on and walk on barefoot, warming up rapidly in sunlight.

Untreated wood varies in color and texture, depending on the source. Without paint, stain, and varnish, this living, breathing material weathers to give a gentle, unobtrusive finish, the subtle grain patterns becoming more apparent with age. It takes on an altogether different character when wet. If you want to color decking, a pale gray stain will enhance the natural shade rather than masking it completely. Varnish brings out the color of the wood, but can look artificial and requires frequent maintenance.

Decking can be the solution to a number of design problems. It can be used to create a sympathetic and natural-looking surface over solid concrete in a courtyard or atrium. It can transform a roof space that has load-bearing restrictions when constructed as a suspended floor. It can provide a

level seating area on a sloping site and can create different levels with stepped sections on a flat site. Use decking to floor a veranda or to provide a sitting area projecting over water or a sea of gravel.

CHOOSING THE WOOD

Unfortunately, most softwood decking is not suitable for damp, shady sites, especially in high rainfall areas, because it quickly becomes covered in slippery algae. You can buy decking that has been mechanically scored to give greater grip, but it does not look as natural as smooth-planed planks. On boardwalks used to traverse shady areas or damp stretches over water, cover planks with chicken wire for extra grip.

Buy wood from managed woodlands and generally avoid tropical hardwoods. Temperate hardwoods such as oak are far more durable and

above: *This sitting area is a picture of serenity. Decking backed by bold plantings of grasses overhangs a still, reflecting pool.*

right: *Boardwalks work well in more naturalistic settings, such as through woodland or across patches of marshy ground.*

rot-resistant than softwoods such as pine, though one softwood, Western red cedar, contains a resin that resists rot. Buy seasoned wood and check with your local supplier which type of wood is most suitable for your purpose. Reclaimed wood may be a cheaper option and has a ready-aged quality. You may be able to get wider, thicker planks, which give an air of solidity.

CONSTRUCTION

Provided the wood is kept off the ground, with free air circulation beneath the deck, and no part is in permanent contact with damp soil, it will last for years. Wood that has been pressure-treated with preservative will last even longer, but is usually tinted green. Make sure you wear tough, water-proof gloves when handling treated wood, as the fungicide may be toxic.

Wood is a very versatile construction material that can be cut to any shape with the right equipment. Decks can be designed with flowing lines and gentle curves as well as the more usual rectilinear pattern. If you feel the task is beyond your ability, consider employing a professional, who will not only have the expertise to cut and join the planks skillfully, but will also know how far apart to place the joists for safety and how to make the concrete supporting piers.

Building boardwalks over bog and water is a job for someone with experience in such matters. Sometimes, especially in wild and woodland gardens, boardwalks are used instead of more conventional paths. In addition to blending in beautifully, they give a little height to the walkway and create a different perspective on the garden. Boardwalks may run through areas of dense, grassy planting to create the illusion of a water garden.

Screens are not solid divisions. If you make a conscious effort, you can often glimpse what is on the other side, which is far more evocative than a direct view—it is the suggestion of something interesting but half hidden that intrigues the visitor. Curiously, even when the gaps are quite large, the eye still tends to focus on the area in front. Screens are useful in a small garden because they let light through and keep the space feeling airy and vibrant.

Screens

In Japan many traditional screens are built from lashed bamboo. Different types are used for specific purposes in and around the garden. For example, *sode-gaki* ("sleeve" fence), a curved lattice framework attached to a wall, may be used to partially screen an area to create a rather more intimate atmosphere. These beautifully designed structures become an integral part of the overall design. An informal bamboo framework may also be used as a backdrop to a water-basin feature, lantern or other ornament, adding emphasis by strengthening the overall composition.

Screens of different materials and designs give the garden a particular character. In the wild or woodland garden, you might try substituting bamboo for loosely woven panels of willow. Although the structure will not last indefinitely, it blends easily with planting and makes a useful temporary backdrop while you wait for shrubs to grow. Screening made from rustic poles would look appropriate in a wild or woodland garden.

Square or rectangular wooden trellis works well in a more structured or architectural setting, especially when the holes are relatively large. Choose sturdy wooden trellis panels that will resist warping and attach to solid posts. Flimsy trellis that undulates in and out creates a feeling of unease. Consider setting each panel into a quite substantial wooden frame. You can also make your own trellis to any simple design using roofing lathes joined together with an industrial staple gun.

Screening is useful for creating dappled shade in a hot sunny spot, and interesting shadow patterns appear on the ground at certain times of the day. Screens also help to filter and deflect wind. Solid boundaries tend to create even more turbulence in a windy site, wreaking havoc with delicate plants. A temporary solution is to attach black woven plastic

above: Hazel hurdles have an organic feel and work particularly well in more informal situations such as wild, woodland, and country gardens.

above: *A treillage (decorative trellis) screen of Oriental design enhances the look of the garden while providing an effective division.*

mesh to the back of the trellis panel using a staple gun. Fitted behind the trellis, the mesh is surprisingly unobtrusive and can be removed when it has done its job. This arrangement could also provide shade for sun-sensitive plants and humans.

You can build an inexpensive screen suitable for boundaries using wooden fence planks. Construct a framework of upright posts set into the ground

with concrete or using metal sockets. Make a horizontal framework with struts going across the top and bottom of the uprights. Nail vertical planks to this framework, leaving gaps between to let in the light. Stout bamboo poles can also be set into the ground, with or without lashed cross-pieces, to create a light screen. Well-behaved clump-forming bamboo, such as many belonging to the genus *Phyllostachys* or *Fargesia,* can be planted to create a living screen. Each year, thin by removing the oldest growth and errant shoots to keep a graceful look.

Solid Backdrops

Garden boundaries are often marked by a solid wall, fence, or hedge, which create privacy and security. Front gardens are frequently open plan; otherwise, boundaries are often kept low and used mainly to define the space. This is rarely the case in Japan, where privacy is a sign of status.

The choice of boundary may be linked to the style, period, and construction material of the house and the kinds of materials in common use in the locality. In the Zen garden a smooth plastered wall will blend with many different styles. This could be built relatively cheaply using breezeblocks hidden by a coating of cement and finished with slate or terracotta tile coping. Painting the wall using one of the earth tones like soft terracotta gives the look of traditional Japanese rammed earth walls. A gentle gray could also blend well with the surroundings. Pure white is an option for a modern minimalist garden and for lightening shady spots, but beware, in full sun the glare can be somewhat aggressive.

A totally plain wall would make the perfect backdrop for a dry garden of rock and gravel or a large rectangular pool in a minimalist garden. In a more naturalistic setting, you could build a dry stone wall using rough blocks, or cement them together for a somewhat smoother finish. Alternatively, to give a breezeblock wall a more organic feel, work flints, cobblestones, or sections of pantile into the cement.

FENCING

A fence is generally a cheaper option than a wall, but the design of ready-made panels tends to be limited. A simple option is to nail wooden planks to a supporting frame, as described on page 71, but leaving no gaps. To create a Japanese feel, you could also use square trellis panels painted dark brown or black with split bamboo fencing stapled to the reverse. Hazel or willow hurdles work well in a wild or woodland setting but, like bamboo, need to be replaced roughly every ten years. Avoid stains and other wood treatments in bright garish colors—they will jar the senses. Most supposedly authentic wood colors look artificial; wooden fencing is best untreated or stained neutral black or dark brown.

HEDGING

Hedges need a lot more maintenance, but are useful for marking the transition from a stylized or architectural part of the garden to an area with a more natural feel. Clipped formal hedges act like green architecture, having many of the qualities of dressed stone, and associate well with buildings. Hedging plants with smaller leaves, such as yew and box, give a finer surface after clipping, creating a less distracting foil than varieties with broader leaves, such as holly (*Ilex aquifolium*) and bay (*Laurus nobilis*). Hornbeam and beech are both deciduous hedge varieties, but retain coppery leaves through winter and are relatively fast growing. For the Zen garden simple clipped designs are best— perpendicular sides or ones cut with a slight angle and a perfectly flat top. Small openings can be cut into walls and hedges to give a tantalizing glimpse of the garden beyond.

right: The boundary formed by this red earth wall is given extra emphasis by the raised bed filled with clipped balls.

In the Zen garden a series of gateways is sometimes used gradually to prepare a person mentally and spiritually so they can experience the heart of the garden in the right frame of mind. The area used to achieve this transformation may be very small, but between each gateway the character of the garden or pathway changes subtly, bringing you closer to a state of mindfulness with each step.

Gates and Entranceways

above: *Although this wooden gateway blends into its woodland setting, on passing through it you would be aware of a subtle transition.*

The process reminds me of the way my teacher prepares us for our yoga class. When we first enter the room, we are very much connected to the outside world. We sit on the floor, but we are still chatting and catching up on the news. Then we hear the first "ting" as the little metal meditation cymbals are struck against each other. We all stop talking and listen intently. The second "ting" comes and, eyes closed, we follow the ringing sound for as long as we can. Just as it has faded to nothingness, she strikes the cymbals a third and final time. As the sound fades we are aware that our breathing has become slow and steady. We are ready to continue.

This process of calming the mind is an essential part of the tea ceremony. Here guests pass through an outer gate, which is then locked behind them. They assemble at the *koshikake machiai* (roofed waiting bench), in an ornamental garden that is obviously manmade. When summoned, they pass though a middle gate and into the inner garden. The tea garden is imbued with the qualities of *wabi* (solitude among nature) and *sabi* (an atmosphere of age). As they silently move through further gateways, the garden becomes wilder, symbolizing the gradual letting go of worldly cares as they draw closer to nature. Passing through the *chumon* (inner gate), the guest walks the *roji* (dewy path), the final stage. It is like a rough mountain track leading to a hermit's hut.

Roofed gateways add greater emphasis and importance to an entrance. In Japan they are simply covered in thatch, shingles, or wooden boards, and have the added bonus of providing a visitor with temporary shelter from the rain. In Japanese monasteries, a roofed gate once led to an empty courtyard, which was crossed to reach the *hojo* (main hall). When they fell out of use, these courtyards became the first temple gardens.

Even when not roofed as such, gates often have a simple framework around them with a horizontal bar overhead. This makes you more conscious of having passed through to a different place. Gates in a boundary fence or wall can be tall and solid so that they screen the garden from the outside world, or an open lattice framework, perhaps made from bamboo. This weave effect prevents a small, enclosed area from feeling claustrophobic and allows you to catch a glimpse of the garden as you pass by.

SMOOTH TRANSITIONS

A gate across a pathway can be purely symbolic, with no fence or barrier on either side to prevent access. The gate may consist of a simple wood and bamboo framework. It is important that the transition from one area to the next is made with sensitivity. The transition into the garden may be eased by mirroring the design of paving and planting on either side of the entrance. A large stone on each side of the boundary might emphasize the importance of stepping across. Similarly, a roofed veranda or climber-covered arbor creates a gentle, semishaded transition zone when moving from the relatively shady interior of the house to the sunny garden.

above: *The solid wall and massive stone gate effectively block the view through to the next area of garden, creating an air of mystery.*

The Tea House

Apart from verandas, there are few constructions that could be considered typical of the Zen garden, though the tea house is a significant element of the traditional roji.

Built at the end of the *roji* (dewy path), the tea house was modeled on a simple hermit's retreat. Here participants in the tea ceremony find a *tsukubai* (water basin), and kneeling down, the guests ritually purify body and mind. As a reminder of the flow of the seasons, the host may place a fall leaf or a spring blossom on the ground.

Having walked slowly through the *roji* to get to this point, the guests will have already drawn their awareness within themselves. When asked to enter, they remove their shoes and crouch through a low doorway. The door is closed, blocking the garden from view. Everyone taking part in the ceremony does so with purity of intent.

Inside the guests may be shown an *ikebana* arrangement or a scroll painting. They then sit on the *tatami* mats and the ceremony begins. The host makes green tea, going through an elaborate and carefully executed series of elegant movements. Each person sips from the same simple bowl. The ceremony over, the host and guests may speak quietly, perhaps discussing art or flower arranging.

OTHER BUILDINGS

Over time the tea gardens, particularly the dewy path elements, were often condensed and symbolically re-created in small courtyard gardens, with stepping-stone paths that were never intended to be walked on.

TSUKUBAI ARRANGEMENT

Where the tsukubai is used in the tea ceremony, carefully selected stones are placed around the water basin in a traditional arrangement similar to the one shown above. The large flat stone is for guests to kneel on as they bend to scoop up water in their hands. The smaller stones on each side are for the guest's belongings, and this is also where the host might place a single flower or leaf. In the center of the arrangement is a cobblestone drain. The basin continually refills with fresh water. This water is also used to make the tea during the ceremony.

There might not be room to re-create a traditional tea hut in your garden, but you could convert a wooden summerhouse with a few simple cosmetic changes, or create the right feel by applying a rustic façade to the tool shed. Or you could make a sitting area with a raised wooden platform, pitched roof, and heavy supporting beams.

Sunrooms, conservatories, covered verandas, and pergolas are all potentially valuable transitional areas between house and garden. Often they are too ornate for the Zen garden, but you could paint a conservatory black or dark brown to help it recede into the background. In the Zen garden, simple rectilinear summerhouses and conservatories work best. Split bamboo shades on the outside of the glass help the structure blend in. Screen the building from the garden or incorporate it into the design.

Silently sitting

by the window.

Leaves fall

and flowers bloom.

The *seasons* come and go.

Could there be

a better *life*?

backed for long periods, perhaps in meditation, will find that a bench or stool will suffice. But most people will benefit from back support of some kind and a cushion for extra comfort. You do not have to spend a lot of money to have suitable seating for the Zen garden. A simple bench made from a solid plank of untreated wood supported on bricks or breezeblocks will do just fine. To make it more esthetically pleasing, wire the blocks together, cover them with chicken wire, and coat with a layer of stiff cement. Before it dries, texture the cement so it looks like stone.

Outdoor furniture is often used to create a focal point in Western gardens, but in a Zen space, seating usually blends unobtrusively into the

Seating and Garden Furniture

Whether you are taking a break from weeding or slipping out for a few moments of quiet contemplation, you need a place to sit. Some all-weather seating is essential; if you have to get a chair out of storage, you are unlikely to sit out when the mood takes you, and you could miss so much that way. Position seating with great care, making sure you have the desired outlook—by the pond; across a particularly pleasing stretch of garden; to an ornament framed by planting. You may want to sit in seclusion, or somewhere that catches the last rays of sunlight at the end of the day.

FURNITURE DESIGN
Choose a piece of furniture that suits the way you want to sit. Anyone practiced at sitting straight-

background. If it is permanently positioned, it should have an air of substance, almost as though it has grown up out of the ground. Solidly built wooden furniture and benches made from stone will do just that, especially when weathered. A flat-topped rock or a section of tree trunk at a suitable height for sitting would also make a useful temporary perch. Because they are so durable, hardwoods like oak and iroko are ideal for permanent seating; an occasional oil treatment will keep them in good condition. Softwood furniture needs regular maintenance to prevent rotting if it is left outside permanently, but is relatively cheap to buy. At the

right: Simple wooden furniture blends with the decking. Privacy and shade is provided by the saillike canopy of canvas.

other end of the spectrum from organic-feeling wood and wicker furniture is metal and glass. The latter work best with modern architecture in a highly minimalist setting.

A couple of lightweight folding chairs made from metal and wooden slats will provide flexible seating. Painted dark green or black, they almost disappear against foliage and are easy to pick up and move to wherever you want to sit. Canvas-covered bucket seats or director's chairs are also suitable. They have plain, unfussy lines and are surprisingly comfortable. It is lovely to stretch out on a deck or lawn when the weather is good, so keep on hand some rush mats or rugs and large outdoor cushions. These can also be used for meditation.

DINING OUTSIDE

An outdoor dining area is best screened off from the Zen garden so as not to disturb the special atmosphere, but the style of the furniture can still be in keeping. For a place to sit and eat for all the family, consider a simple wooden picnic table with bench seats. If you dine Eastern style, sitting on cushions on the ground, your table needs to be a low square or rectangle. Such a table could be made from a rectangular piece of stone or slate supported centrally by a column of building blocks (these will be hidden from view). It could be functional or decorative, perhaps used to display some beautiful shells or pebbles, a piece of driftwood, a vase of flowers, or a bonsai tree.

You may have to search long and hard to find a decorative item that will work in your Zen-inspired space. A well-designed garden should need few ornaments. Zen gardeners are less concerned with decoration for its own sake because they are aware that nature is producing countless works of art in the garden every day.

Sculptural Form

In Zen, the garden can be seen on many different levels. It is a composition in the artistic sense, with the various elements arranged to be pleasing to the eye. It is also a symbolic representation of nature, a distillation, if you will, that rejects anything that is not essential to creating that view. However, it may even go one stage farther and become almost completely abstract.

Zen philosophy challenges the way we perceive things, our view of reality, and can be very provocative. Although not in the least traditional in terms of Japanese garden design, in the Zen garden it would not seem out of place to see unadorned mirrors or an object with a mirrored surface such as a polished metal sphere. Neither would it be great a surprise to see a piece of surreal sculpture, or a modernist water feature. If you were to ask a Zen gardener why they have used a particular object and what it is meant to represent, they would be quite likely to reply that there is no reason, no meaning, it just *is*.

With time the artificial *disappears* And only the natural *remains*

Anything that produces contrast in color or form inevitably draws the eye and creates a focus within the garden, for example, a red-leaved maple in fall set against a clipped green hedge. At a more abstract level you might choose a water-worn boulder or a large block of weathered wood as the point of contrast in an area of pure gravel.

Ornaments that we traditionally associate with Japanese gardens—stone water basins, stone lanterns, bamboo deer-scarers—all began life as functional objects. The lanterns in particular have become more stylized and ornate with time, and only the plainest would feature in a Zen garden. Zen takes a practical, down-to-earth view of life, and something that is inherently ornamental but is also potentially useful would be favored over something that was purely decorative—a weathered copper basin, a woven hazel obelisk, a plain ceramic water jar, an old metal bell, and so on. Wind chimes of bamboo, wood, or

metal can also be ornamental, creating different tones depending on the material from which they are made. Hang them from tree branches or from the eaves of a building, veranda, or arbor.

PERSONAL TOUCH

If you are still wondering what to use in a particular space, look for something that means something to you or provokes an emotional response even if it just leaves you feeling calm and relaxed every time your eye settles on it—a sculpture with a serene expression perhaps, or an abstract piece with gentle curves that creates a pleasing contrast between light and shadow.

In a relaxed, less stylized setting such as might be found in a wild or woodland garden, you might use something quite organic, like an abstract or figurative wicker or wooden sculpture. Animals or the elements are both likely to be the inspiration for sculpture.

RAW FINISH

Whatever object you choose as a focus, it should have a very simple line and an inherently strong and enduring feel. Choose materials that weather and develop a patina of age, such as metals like copper, brass, and iron that react with the atmosphere. Unglazed terracotta is also a good choice. Avoid paints, varnishes, glazes, and so on that disguise an object's natural beauty.

far left: Stone spheres have a purity of form that works well in a Zen space, and would contrast beautifully with filigree foliage.

left: This weathered stone jar has all the qualities of a piece of natural stone and is just the right scale for the space it occupies.

The placing of a sculptural form has a major effect on how well it performs as a focal point. It can be highly visible or almost half-hidden, depending on the way you set the stage for it. In a wild, secret garden, you may want an ornament to look as though it has been there long enough for the vegetation to have almost reclaimed the spot.

Creating a Focus

Small objects may seem out of proportion in a large space, but can still be used if given the proper emphasis. For example, you could raise the object up above ground level by placing it on a simple plinth. A totally plain plinth of dressed stone or smooth-faced concrete is ideal for highlighting a natural object; a plinth with a textured surface is good for highly polished metal objects. The latter also look well on contrasting raw wooden plinths.

above: *The rounded form of these beach pebbles, arranged in a niche, is emphasized by the straight lines and smoothness of the wall.*

Another way to raise small objects closer to eye level and give them greater emphasis is to create a shelf that juts out from a wall or fence. A *tokonoma* (niche) similar to those traditionally used inside Japanese houses could be created for an ornament, either in a wall, solid fence, or clipped hedge.

A technique used in *ikebana* is to place a plain screen behind the ornament so that all the emphasis is thrown on to the object, clearing away any distractions. Outdoors this could be as simple as a perfectly cut rectangle of slate or natural wood. You could also paint or cover the inside of a niche in a neutral shade that gives maximum contrast for the object.

COMPOSITION AND FUNCTION

Be logical about where you place decorative elements that are also useful. The water basin stands at an entrance for the use of visitors, and a stone lantern lights the way even if it is never actually used for that purpose. Composition is everything. Try to mirror the shape of the ornament in some way. An example might be an arching branch of an overhanging tree or the outline of a clipped shrub in the background reflecting the curve of a large ceramic pot. If the ornament seems to be "floating" out in the open within a very plain area, "anchor" it by adding some planting at the base. Plant sword-shaped or ferny leaves next to a rounded ornament and foliage with a rounded form next to a piece with rectilinear lines. Carefully selected cobblestones and pebbles placed on one side of the object could also be used for this purpose. An object can be emphasized by planting a light framework of bamboo poles as a backdrop: this effectively stops the eye from going beyond the object and adds to the total composition.

Foliage backdrops work well for most garden ornaments, but leaves must be plain, not variegated, and either darker or lighter than the object in front. Small-leaved evergreens such as box or yew are a good choice since they do not overwhelm objects and they generate a feeling of serenity.

ADDING EMPHASIS

The illustration shows a number of techniques for adding weight to an object. The small stone lantern is raised up on a large flat stone, which gives it greater prominence, and a series of stones which increase in size act like steps leading up to it. A dwarf pine softens the whole scene and provides a contrasting backdrop. Finally, a light framework of bamboo stakes prevents the eye wandering beyond the composition, thus keeping the focus on the lantern.

Lighting

Many poems are written in praise of the moon and the garden at night. In Zen, the moon represents the true nature of things, and seeing the moon reflected in still or rippled water is especially symbolic and thought provoking. The garden at nighttime can be a magical place to sit and listen to nocturnal creatures, to drink in the fragrance of night-scented flowers, or to simply gaze up at the stars in the sky.

Unfortunately, even when the moon is full, it cannot be relied on to illuminate the garden, so some other form of lighting is needed to guide your way. Whenever you are designing a lighting plan, try to emulate the subtle effects of moonlight—the way it throws shadows onto paths and walls, reflects in any patch of water, and the way it causes pale-colored blooms to glow.

For a terrace or courtyard adjacent to the house, avoid spotlights that are angled to shine down onto the area from above. They can be dazzling if you accidentally look straight at them. An arbor built out from the wall will provide useful mounting points for lighting. Tiny white mini lights woven through a climber produce a delicate effect reminiscent of starlight. Alternatively, you could hang small candle lanterns from the crosspieces or from surrounding trees. Another soft way to light a seating area is to set garden candles in ordinary earthenware pots in among the plants at ground level. Citronella candles are useful next to seats because they discourage mosquitoes. Smoke coils, incense, and smudge sticks are similarly effective.

If the garden has a Japanese feel, then a traditional stone lantern could be used for its original purpose; a candle or oil lamp inside evokes just the right mood. In a contemporary Western setting, other lantern designs made from ceramic, reconstituted stone, or terracotta could be used. A lantern placed next to a pool creates a beautiful reflection, and on still evenings you could even float a few candles on the water.

Mini uplighters at ground level can be angled to cast a gentle light onto individual rocks, trees, ornaments, and specimen plants, accentuating their sculptural form. Their light can also be directed onto garden structures such as arbors, emphasizing architectural features. Painted black, these small lights are relatively unobtrusive during daytime, but if you want to hide the light casing altogether, you can install uplighters flush with the ground. This type of light should be built into paths and decks at the time of construction. Always employ a qualified electrician if you are at all unsure.

right: The shape and texture of this stone lantern is subtly highlighted by a concealed mini spotlight set into the ground.

As the *heart* finds the

Changeless

It emits a natural light

Which *illumines* all

Which is still false

Planting

On seeing the *peach* flowers

Abbot Rei-Un became *enlightened*

As did Master Kyo-Gen

At *hearing* the crack of a bamboo

Spring

After the austerity of winter, we cannot help but be cheered by the sight of blossom in early spring. Unlike later flowering trees, where the blooms are mixed with leaves, the plum, the apricot, and the almond all flower on bare branches, as if to emphasize their precociousness. Many evergreens are used in Zen gardens, but without some deciduous trees and shrubs, they would feel too static.

At this important turning point in the year, it is good to have at least one spring-flowering tree. Few evergreens have the delicacy of deciduous trees. Blossom does not have to upset the calm atmosphere though. An early-blossoming tree that produces masses of tiny single blooms along its slender branches could be planted in the corner of a moss garden. It will provide a temporary focus and will fade into the background as soon as the leaves appear. On a smaller scale, you could plant a group of crocus at the base of a sunny hedge, or some primroses through a carpet of moss.

FIRST SIGNS

The signs of spring appear very early in the season if you take the time to look for them. An invisible life force is at work, swelling buds and pushing shoots up through the ground. Walking slowly around the garden, really looking at the plants with each step you take, you will find every day is a journey of discovery. Even if you can see blossom from the window, how can you experience its fragrance or appreciate the delicate beauty of its fragile flowers unless you go outside to visit it? Spring flowers arrive at a precarious time. Warm spells encourage them to open, perhaps too early, and then suddenly the temperature drops and they

are no more. With the first warm rays of sunshine, the early insects appear and begin foraging. The intermittent buzz of the bumblebee makes a welcome return. The pond becomes alive with croaking frogs and, in colder regions, hibernating animals begin to emerge from their winter sleep.

Moment after *moment*
Everything comes out of
Nothingness
This is the true joy of life

Birdsong changes noticeably; the forlorn melodies of winter are abandoned and replaced by vibrant declarations of territory and readiness to mate. Changes happen slowly at first, and then as the weather improves, life burgeons apace. Leaves unfurl almost overnight, and flower buds seem to pop all at once.

right: *The delicate blossom of* Prunus mume *'Beni-chidori' heralds the onset of spring in the Zen garden.*

Summer

As spring becomes summer, an atmosphere of calm descends on the garden. Warmer temperatures and longer evenings encourage us to linger and we make more time to sit, watch, and contemplate. We stand outside on summer nights star-gazing and get up early to experience the freshness of a summer's day dawning. It is cooler to work early or late in the day, leaving the middle free to sit in a shady spot close to the sound of running water.

In Japan, summer is symbolized by the green of willow foliage, and the weeping willow, although certainly not a tree for the smaller garden, does create a picture in the mind's eye of indolent summer days. But there is activity—if we choose to listen and observe. The water garden is a good place to start. In the pond the fish are much more visible, lying close to the surface, basking in the warmer water, occasionally snapping at an unsuspecting fly. Frogs lie well camouflaged, moving only to feed or when disturbed. The water is criss-crossed by insect traffic, drawing in dragonflies that perch momentarily on the water iris before zooming off with a metallic flash. In the evening, bats appear silhouetted in the still-light sky, darting across the pool as they hunt for night-flying moths. Birds cautiously come to drink and bathe in between nest building and feeding their young. The air is filled with their chattering, and liquid song.

IMPERMANENCE

As we watch ephemeral butterflies flitting from flower to flower, sipping nectar as though they do not have a care in the world, we are reminded of our own brief time here on earth. We tend to behave as though we will always have tomorrow, and it is a valuable lesson to observe the insects' short-lived existence. Flowers also repeat the message of impermanence, especially ones like the morning glory (*Ipomea tricolor*), where each bloom opens at breakfast and may be over by lunch.

TRANQUIL GREEN

The Zen garden is complete without flowers; in fact, too many different colors and forms create distraction and a feeling of discord. Green often dominates, even in summer, looking vibrant against the rocks and gravel. And as we develop our sensitivity, we come to appreciate how many shades there are. When flowers do open, they are vibrant against the greenery: a spot of hot red or orange can create a strong focus. Neutral-colored flowers come and go in the background, never fighting for attention, only softly enhancing the scene.

Summer light can be quite harsh, and dappled shade makes a welcome retreat from the glare. In warm weather the doors and windows are flung open, and the division between indoors and out disappears. The garden may need watering, a job for the cool of an evening. It is wonderful to smell the damp earth and see the rocks and plants glisten.

right: These tender moisture-loving arum lilies (Zantedeschia rehmannii) produce their sculptural blooms in vibrant colors.

Fall

This season, perhaps the most atmospheric of all, steeped in images of death and decay, represents the very essence of mushin—*the transience of human existence. It may be a contemplative period for the Zen gardener, but fall is not a depressing time. There is so much beauty in death, and by way of contrast this is also a time of abundance, with all kinds of fruits and berries ripening.*

As the days shorten and the nights grow colder, all of nature knows that winter is approaching. Animals and birds prepare for lean times ahead, some fattening up in readiness for hibernation. There is a burst of activity, an urgency to their movement. Insects become scarcer, the background hum of summer barely audible now. Some find nooks and crannies in which to overwinter, for others, their brief existence is nearly at an end. Accepting the natural order of things is fundamental to Zen.

BEAUTY IN CHAOS

Fall can seem an untidy season for those who seek order in their lives, but one of life's certainties is that things change. Sometimes, by rigidly sticking to our view of perfection, we are unable to see the beauty in everyday situations. A traditional tale illustrates the point well.

There was once a priest who was busily preparing the temple garden for the arrival of some guests, whom he wanted to impress. As he worked, sweeping the leaves, picking up every last twig and fallen seedpod, and even combing some of the mosses, an old master watched him from the adjoining property. "What do you think of the garden?" asked the priest when he had finished, barely able to disguise the note of pride and satisfaction in his voice. "Oh, it's very good, very good," replied the master, "just one thing missing, I think, but if you'd help me over this wall, I'll put it right for you." Out of deference to the old man, he did as he was bid, and the master made his way

When things *flourish* they begin to decline
At midday the *sun* starts to set
When the moon is done waxing
It starts to wane

over to a tree at the center of the garden which was almost ready to drop its leaves. He shook the trunk firmly, and instantly the mossy carpet and pathways were covered in a random patterning of leaves. "There, that's better," he said to the astonished priest.

In fall, the light is softer and has a golden quality that enhances the reds, oranges, and yellows of deciduous leaves, fruits, and berries. As the season moves on, a morning mist often lingers, dew covers the ground, and cobwebs sparkle. The gardener's work continues in a relaxed way. Raking leaves can turn from a chore into a serene moving meditation. It is said that in fall, sweeping is left to boys and old men, knowing they will not be too rigorous!

above: A single deciduous tree can transform the fall garden. Here scarlet red maple leaves make a startling contrast with moss.

left: The fallen leaves of a tulip tree cover the ground with a carpet of gold. Do not rush to sweep them away!

93

Winter

In winter in Japan, northern regions and the mountains become covered in snow, and the natural landscape is exquisitely beautiful. In temperate latitudes, winter has many faces and can vary from uncharacteristic mildness to frost and biting winds that take your breath away. We marvel at the sight of minute ice sculptures created by frost or at a fresh carpet of snow glowing in the moonlight.

Endurance is a favorite theme in Japan, and winter's harsh weather conditions test nature to her limits. It is not surprising that the Japanese chose two of the strongest and most resilient plants, the bamboo and the pine, to symbolize their New Year.

Observing the natural world in the garden at this time provides us with strategies that can be applied to our own lives, and shows that we all have the potential to survive situations of great adversity. Zen teaches that flexibility and patience are qualities that can help us to weather any storm. In addition, from a clear mind uncluttered by the debris of thoughts and emotions comes wisdom, and this enables us to act in the right way in any given situation.

The austerity of winter can make this a sobering season, but the quietness experienced in the garden at this time and the simplicity of

A student of *Zen*

Should learn how

to read

The *love* letters

Sent by the *snow*,

The *wind* and the rain

a monochrome landscape created by heavy frost, snow or fog, offers the opportunity for contemplation without distraction. Then, winter becomes a metaphor for life without complexity. Just as the glassy surface of a pond reflects an undistorted picture, so simplifying our lives and clearing our minds can enable us to realize the true nature of our own existence.

In mild areas, a quiet backdrop of evergreens will create continuity, reminding us that life goes on no matter what. Here it is possible to grow a few flowers, a symbol that spring is waiting in the wings—a touch of yang in the yin of winter. Early bulbs such as snowdrops, herbaceous plants including the sculptural hellebores, shrubs, and trees can be used to sprinkle a flower or two among the greenery, but the emphasis is on moderation. Winter is a quiet period, symbolizing purity and restraint. Fortunately, most winter flowers are quite subtle, and many make up for small size and muted color with a

left: Perennial foliage contributes to the winter scene; do not clear it too early. Evergreens like this bergenia are especially valuable. below: Frozen in time—frost crystals transform this early blossom into an exquisite ice sculpture.

delicious perfume. In a sheltered garden you can often detect a winter-flowering shrub in advance of seeing it. The witch hazels (*Hamamelis*) with their spidery flowers, the evergreen *Daphne odora*, and sweet box (*Sarcococca*) are just some of the fragrant delights to be found in the winter garden. During winter you will appreciate the care you have taken to create views from the house, but spending time in the garden will provide renewed inspiration!

Planting Philosophy

One of the central themes of Zen is the fleeting nature of our existence—death as an inevitable part of life. We are reminded of this transformation when we observe plants going through their natural cycle. In the West we artificially extend the growing season from early spring to late fall. The miraculous sight of a bud opening to reveal its bloom is often masked by the competition. By contrast, Zen gardens use a high proportion of evergreens, and seasonal changes take place against this green backdrop. A break is left between the various flowering and foliage highlights so that each can be appreciated in isolation: the four seasons are celebrated and the natural order followed.

NATURE DISTILLED

The Zen garden does not try to reproduce the natural landscape: rather it tries to evoke the essence of nature. There may be very few plants in the garden, but to the onlooker a single tree could represent a woodland, and iris leaves vegetation around the edge of a lake. Each plant is placed with care, being mindful of the size to which it will finally grow, the effect of light on the foliage, and how it will look in that position at different times of year.

In the West, beauty is often acclaimed only when it represents our narrow view of perfection, but in Zen, beauty is seen to exist beyond the conventional interpretation—the faded flower, the fallen leaf. Age does not diminish beauty—it often enhances it—and a flower is of no lesser value because its petals lie scattered on the ground. In Zen gardens, plants are chosen for their understated beauty and their architectural qualities, and the most natural-looking forms of plants are favored. A plant should still have something to add to the garden scene even in its quiet period.

Smaller subjects are always planted in groups of three, five, or any other odd number—a swathe of the same plant is dramatic and naturalistic. Try to imagine your garden as a black-and-white photograph so you can study its overall form and texture without the distraction of color.

STRUCTURE

A strong framework of permanent planting is essential. Even in a tiny courtyard, plant a small tree (a maple in a container perhaps), a carefully pruned bamboo, or clipped box. In addition to contrasting the different leaf shapes, think about setting tall upright plants against those that give a horizontal impression producing a rhythm of masses and voids. Do not be too rigid, though—a tuft of upright stems rising out of low groundcover makes an interesting accent. You can often utilize a plant's natural habit to enhance certain situations. For example, the arching stems of angel's fishing rods (*Dierama*) look wonderful cascading gracefully over a pool. Large-leaved plants, and ones with grassy foliage can help to create the illusion of water when combined with a dry cobbled stream.

Choose plants that do not need staking, and avoid silverlings and plants that suggest a hot, dry climate. They will tend to jar with the cool green mossiness of the Zen garden.

right: The sight of morning glory flowers, which last for just a single day, reminds us of the need to live life in the moment.

Shall I compare this life

To a *lightning* flash

Or a drop of *dew*?

Even as I speak

It has *passed*

Foliage as Sculpture

The leaves of certain plants look as though they have been crafted by an artist. Think of the sublime curves of the hosta leaf, its parallel veins converging at the tapering tip. These "architectural" plants work well adjacent to man-made constructions, especially modern, minimalist-style buildings. Sculptural foliage has a special place in the Zen garden because simplicity and purity of line are so highly valued. These plants often have enough presence to stand alone in the garden and may be seen as living sculptures. A mature Japanese maple with its twisted arching limbs and exquisite leaves is a lovely example. And the beauty is that this kind of natural artwork is constantly changing.

Living sculptures need space and a simple backdrop to really shine. Set them beside an expanse of gravel, within paving, or at the edge of a lawn. Water also makes a good foil. By the pool among low ground cover, try a solitary towering specimen of the giant ornamental rhubarb (*Rheum palmatum* 'Atrosanguineum'), its large, jaggedly cut leaves, each perfectly angled, surmounting the spearlike flower stem. *Gunnera manicata* is even more impressive here, but can only be accommodated in large gardens. The leaves are enormous, and each has a superstructure of veins that are reminiscent of steel girders.

In contrast to these broad shapes are the swordlike leaves of plants like iris and New Zealand flax (*Phormium tenax*). They provide a strong vertical accent to contrast with horizontal plantings and structures such as decks. Ornamental grasses and sedges, plants such as day lily, crocosmia, and agapanthus also have narrow leaves, but they arch over gracefully. Straight or curving, this kind of foliage is wonderfully complemented by rounded forms—smooth cobblestones or the leaves of plants like bergenia and certain hostas, and the almost circular foliage of *Darmera peltata*. Ferns show the finest workmanship. The crosier shape of the new frond unfurling has a mathematical purity,

and the filigree structure of the expanded leaf balances heavier foliage and stone beautifully.

Bamboos have an undeniably Eastern quality. Taller clump-forming kinds, such as those belonging to the genus *Phyllostachys,* make particularly fine specimens. Bamboos are sculptural through and through, from the shape of the leaf blade to the way the branches are arranged in whorls and the arching habit of the culm, or stem.

Some shrubs and trees have very large, leathery, evergreen foliage that contrast well with filigree types. Two with oblong-shaped leaves are the Bull bay (*Magnolia grandiflora*), which also has beautifully sculpted flowers, and *Viburnum rhytidophllum*. The glossy leaves of *Fatsia japonica* are hand-shaped. Acacias and the golden form of the honey locust (*Gleditsia triacanthos* 'Sunburst') have leaves made up of a series of leaflets, appearing frondlike and rather delicate. The Japanese angelica tree (*Aralia elata*) has the same leaf structure, but on a much bigger scale. Sometimes it is the way the branches are arranged that gives the plant an eye-catching structure: the fishbone cotoneaster (*Cotoneaster horizontalis*) has tiny leaves, but the branches make an interesting pattern.

Some hardy climbers have an architectural quality. The golden hop (*Humulus lupulus* 'Aurea'), is an herbaceous climber with lobed leaves of lime green; crimson glory vine (*Vitis coignetiae*) has broad, almost rounded foliage, and the Chinese gooseberry (*Actinidia chinensis*) is also striking.

above: Gunnera manicata *is a giant sculptural plant that is only suitable for planting by pools in large gardens.*

left: *A striking collection of grasses grown in plain terracotta pots gives this decked area a refreshing, contemporary feel.*

The Green Garden

Green has a powerful tranquilizing effect on the nervous system. Think of how you feel after walking though a woodland in midsummer— everything is bathed in a soft green light, the ground is covered in emerald mosses and airy ferns, and even the tree trunks are tinged with green algae. A similar feeling comes from the green garden where predominantly evergreen shrubs, trees, mosses, and groundcover plants are combined to produce a calm, restful outdoor environment.

Many evergreen plants are shade tolerant, and shade seems to enhance the depth of their greenness. Broad-leaved evergreens have a slightly heavy feel which, when combined with large uncut pieces of rock, creates an air of permanence. After only a few years, the garden can look as though it has been in existence forever—a welcome contrast to our constantly changing and fast-moving lives.

EVERGREEN COLOR
However, such gardens do change, if only very subtly, and the Zen gardener learns to focus on those changes. When evergreen shrubs produce fresh foliage, it is always of a different shade and character to the mature leaves. Certain types also may have relatively inconspicuous blooms of green, white, or cream. With *Elaeagnus* × *ebbingei*, for example, the tiny, waxy-white fall flowers are found under a dense covering of leaves, but a deliciously spicy fragrance soon alerts you to their presence.

A combination of broadleaved evergreen shrubs, bamboos, and conifers works particularly well. However a, few

deciduous elements lighten the space and introduce a note of change and seasonality. In winter the bare stems often produce an interesting line or have an architectural framework. Some have textured or patterned bark in various colors. New growth in spring is often colored, and in the fall there are rich tints of purple, red, orange, and yellow.

SUBTLE SHADING
The term green garden is something of a misnomer. Among the true greens can be gray- and blue-greens, leaves with an overall red or purplish cast, yellow- or lime-green-leaved shrubs and ones with variegated leaves. To retain a quiet feel, avoid brightly variegated foliage and include just a few plants with subtle marbling or spotting. Shrubs with yellow leaves may scorch in full sun, and the brightness of the color is tempered by shade. Avoid shrubs with dark purple foliage. These make too strong a contrast and create visual "holes" in the overall framework.

Place plants with care to produce pleasing combinations and contrasts, bearing in mind height and spread, overall habit, texture, and color. Limit the number of plants producing seasonal highlights. When contrasting foliage, think about the different leaf mosaic patterns, the size and shape of the blade, as well as texture and light-reflecting qualities.

left: *The bright-yellow striped bamboo* Pleioblastus auricomus *creates a splash of color.*
right: *Decorative paving adds textural interest to a planting of foliage in this shade garden. Mosslike* Soleirolia *colonizes the crevices.*

Flowers

In our minds, flowers are strongly associated with particular seasons of the year because they display such individual character. In the Zen garden we can grow key plants to emphasize the seasons. An area of snowdrops pushing up through rough grass beneath a bare-stemmed tree says late winter; a peony flowering against the backdrop of a dark evergreen hedge says early summer; and the mauve spikes of lilyturf (*Liriope muscari*) lining a stone path say fall.

CREATIVE PLANTING

In the Zen garden, it is felt that flowers are best appreciated in isolation against a plain foil. That is not to say that flowering combinations are not allowed. Sometimes the most wonderful sights occur spontaneously and should not worry us. It would be wrong to create a garden that was so stiff and restrictive that there was no room for creativity. But keep plantings as simple as possible to retain a feeling of serenity.

Flowers like hydrangea are followed by subtly colored seed heads, which are just as pleasing as the blooms themselves. Large-headed ornamental onions (*Allium*) have such architectural seed heads that they are best grown in isolation or with green diaphanous flowers.

In the Zen garden, purity of form and sculptural qualities are favored: clean, simple lines of leaf and stem, bud and flower. Overlarge or heavy double blooms tend to weigh the plant down and should be avoided. No plant in the Zen garden should need unsightly staking: few plants stay bolt upright in the wild. Allow plants to develop a unique shape influenced by the elements and their own nature.

Flowers in muted shades are usually selected. Green flowers are ideal, but white, cream, and pale yellow add a note of purity when used sparingly against a green foliage backdrop. These colors also seem to glow in the twilight and in the illuminated garden. Gentle blues, mauve, and lavender are receding colors and give the illusion of distance when planted at the back of the garden. They also create an environment supportive of spiritual contemplation. Reds and oranges are highly visible against greenery and should only be used as an occasional accent. In the green garden, a single red bloom becomes an irresistible draw for the eye.

left: An unfurling arum lily (Zantedeschia aethiopica) is like a living sculpture. With its handsome foliage it is ideal for the Zen garden.

right: The iris is traditionally associated with Japanese gardens. There are many kinds to suit a wide variety of garden habitats.

Standing in the presence of a group of thousand-year-old trees can be a humbling experience. The energy they resonate is often tangible, and it can be an awesome feeling to be close to other living beings of such great age. In Zen, age is equated with wisdom and endurance, and in the garden trees symbolize these qualities.

Trees in the Landscape

Most Japanese gardens contain at least one tree, but people often fear that tree roots might damage foundations, or that the tree will grow too large and block out the light. Some kinds of poplar and willow, for example, are only suitable for very large gardens, but if you choose wisely, trees can dramatically enhance the garden scene. Even a small courtyard can usually accommodate a single specimen tree. One of modest proportions with upright branches can actually make the space seem larger because the eye is carried up and away from the boundaries. And the canopy of a spreading tree can seem like an airy roof in an outdoor room.

A tree can provide a seasonal focus—for winter interest, choose a variety with attractively colored bark, ornamental fruits, or a sculptural form that is pleasing even when the branches are bare. A tree in fall leaf can look stunning against a predominantly green backdrop, and of course in spring, Japanese gardens are filled with blossom produced by ornamental plum, apricot, peach, and cherry.

PINES
In Japan there are many native evergreen tree and shrub species, and they are frequently used to engender a feeling of tranquility in the garden. The pine is the best-loved conifer, grown not only for its foliage but also, as with bamboo, for the sound the wind makes in its branches. Some forms are easy to keep small by pruning, and with careful training, a pine tree can be made to appear older, more gnarled, and weather-beaten.

STRENGTHENING PERSPECTIVE
Trees can be positioned to create a feeling of depth, especially if a staggered arrangement is used in which the first tree is planted relatively close to the viewer. Trees also lift a flat site, helping to restore balance by providing vertical emphasis,

contrasting with the strong horizontal lines produced by buildings and fences. In an open sunny site, trees provide welcome relief by creating dappled shade. A view can be framed between two tree trunks, or the head of a tree can block out certain parts and emphasize the remainder. A single specimen rising out of low planting can add weight to a doorway or garden building, especially when the branches arch across the entrance.

The cypress *tree* *Resonates* With the life of The *Universe*

In the symbolic landscape where a distillation of nature is represented by just a few key elements, a tree might be used to represent a whole forest. Small-growing trees that remain in scale with other miniature features are preferred and are pruned to keep the composition balanced. In the dry garden, a rock grouping planted with a tree might represent a wooded island or a tree growing out of a cliff face. One trained as a multistem would strengthen the illusion of a forest.

left: *Mimosa or silver wattle* (Acacia dealbata) *makes a slender, delicate-looking tree, which is ideal for a small sheltered garden.*
right: *The sculptural form of this pine tree has been achieved by careful training—a kind of cloud pruning.*

Pruning and Shaping Plants

There are several reasons for cutting, pruning, and clipping shrubs and trees. In the Zen garden they are often clipped to bring out the most pleasing shape in a plant. Even very neat and compact shrubs occasionally throw out errant shoots that need to be removed, as well as crossing branches that throw the framework out of balance. And when a deciduous shrub becomes congested with lots of thin, weak growth, the underlying shape of branches can be masked. To retain or enhance the plant's esthetic appeal, especially when it is viewed in winter, it is necessary to remove some of these branchlets to expose the main stems, particularly lower down. This refining process can be taken a stage further, looking at the line, the flow of energy if you like, of a particular branch and removing some of the side shoots to emphasize that flow and enhance the plant's inherent beauty. Work slowly, and stand back to check your progress.

Branches can be trained to grow in a particular way, using cane splints and wiring as well as clipping to produce the desired effect—techniques used in the art of bonsai. In the Zen garden, artificiality is avoided, and this kind of training is used principally to emphasize a trend already displayed in the plant. For example, if some of the branches are bending in the same direction, making the plant rather lopsided, the upright shoots could be bent or removed to give the effect of an older, wind-sculpted tree.

PRUNING FOR SHAPE

It is sometimes possible to convert large, dense, rather ungainly shrubs in a mature garden into small elegant trees by going beneath the foliage canopy and exposing the main trunk and a simple framework of supporting branches, raising the main areas of foliage. You can do this with deciduous and evergreen alike, including common laurel, large rhododendrons, and pines. This technique also lets in more light at ground level, making the space feel more airy and less congested. Some shrubs respond well to clipping, and can be coaxed into billowing forms resembling cloud formations, rolling

above: Clipped box squares alternated with gravel and stone create an abstract checkboard pattern in this minimalist garden.
right: A stone lantern nestles among evergreen shrubs clipped into cloudlike mounds. Organic shaping could fit a contemporary garden.

hills, or waves. This contouring of evergreen shrubs like Japanese azaleas, types of box (*Buxus*), and *Ilex crenata*, creates rather abstract forms and makes a good backdrop to a simple pool or a dry rock garden. More structured topiary, such as cloud pruning and the formation of cones and domes, can also be used in the contemporary Zen-style garden.

PRUNING FOR HEALTH

Pruning is necessary to remove dead branches and parts affected by disease or severe insect attack. With quick-growing shrubs, particularly varieties grown for their flowers, you may also need to remove some of the oldest growth periodically to maintain vigor and flowering performance. Plants such as *Buddleia davidii* that require heavy pruning each year are avoided because they look unnatural in their lopped state. You really need to know a little bit about the plant's growth cycle to be able to choose the correct pruning regime. Some shrubs build up dense, twiggy growth in their interiors; it can cut out light and prevent the free flow of air. As dead leaf matter collects, the conditions are perfect for fungal infection. The problem is most severe when shrubs like box are clipped regularly. To prevent problems, after clipping, thin out some of the stems to create a less dense structure—the gaps soon close up.

part five

Plant Portraits

An *orchid* doesn't
Lose its *fragrance*
Just because no one notices
How *good* it smells

Bamboo

Bamboo is immediately identified with Oriental gardens. It is grown not only for its elegant habit and evergreen foliage, but also for the rustling sound the leaves make in the breeze. In the West bamboos have the reputation of being uncontrollable spreaders. The large-leafed Pseudosasa japonica *can get out of hand, but most of the* Phyllostachys *and* Fargesia *species and cultivars make fine specimens, and are easily kept under control.*

Bamboos grow best when sheltered from wind with a plentiful supply of moisture and soil rich in organic matter. This is best applied as a thick mulch in spring. The leaves are rich in silica and some authorities recommend that fallen leaves should be left *in situ* to decompose so the mineral does not become depleted in the soil.

When exposed to too much wind, especially during winter, or when grown on dry, poor soil, the foliage can scorch, and shoots may die off. However, *Phyllostachys bissetii* remains fresh and green even in quite an exposed site on waterlogged clay; it eventually reaches about 15 feet (4.5 meters) in height and forms a large clump once established. Other *Phyllostachys* are far less vigorous, and many prefer the shelter of a tree canopy, provided the soil is deep, rich, and moist. These conditions bring out the beautiful coloring and markings on the culms, which may be golden yellow as in *Phyllostachys aurea*, green and yellow striped in *P. bambusoides* 'Castillonis', or black as in *P. nigra*.

Most bamboos are ideal for growing in shady courtyard gardens. The neat and compact *Fargesia murieliae* 'Simba' would do well in a pot. It forms a dainty-leafed column around 6 feet (1.8 meters) tall. Larger *Phyllostachys* and *Fargesia*, such as the readily available *F. nitida* and *F. murieliae*, may also be grown in very large containers, but could eventually split the sides as the shoots exert an amazing pressure. In a small courtyard, a tall bamboo could be grown in a large concrete container sunk into the ground to restrict its spread. All of these columnar bamboos have a graceful arching habit and look best as specimens next to a horizontal expanse, such as paving, gravel, or a pool. However, if bamboo is planted too close to a pond, its shoots can grow under the liner and puncture it.

PRUNING BAMBOOS

The best way to control established columnar bamboos is to remove unwanted growth when the new shoots spear through the ground in early summer. In a lawn this is easily achieved by mowing the shoots off. Columnar bamboos, like *Fargesia* and *Thamnocalamus*, must be regulary thinned to avoid highly congested plants.

Some bamboos make low spreading clumps. For variegated green and yellow striped leaves try *Pleioblastus auricomus* or the green and white striped *P. variegatus*. Both produce better-quality foliage when cut down in spring and mulched.

right: Thamnocalamus spathaceus *provides a backdrop for a lantern. This bamboo must be thinned to reveal its beauty.*

Ground Cover

A dense carpet of plants will suppress weed growth and will make an attractive foil for larger specimens. It is important to select ground cover of appropriate vigor and height for the situation you have in mind; otherwise, the plants could spread beyond their allotted space and smother their neighbors. Next to gravel, beware of prolific self-seeders like lady's mantle (Alchemilla mollis) and carpeters that root where they touch the ground.

Plants of differing habit can be used to produce a range of effects. For example, when a small area of low planting is needed to contrast with strongly upright foliage, a group of clump-forming plants with arching leaves could be used. The green and yellow striped evergreen sedge *Carex oshimensis* 'Evergold' is ideal: it has a distinctly Oriental feel, typical of most of the genus, and is easy to care for given reasonably moisture-retentive soil. With their narrow leaves, sedges and ornamental grasses work

above: Well-pruned low-growing junipers look at home with rock and gravel, and make superb evergreen ground cover.

well with round or broad-leaved plants like bergenia and the creeping bronze-leaved carpeter *Ajuga reptans* 'Catlin's Giant' as well as with pebbles and cobblestones. The soft hummocks of the Japanese grass *Hakonechloa macra* 'Aureola' are banded with clear yellow and, in dappled shade, combine perfectly with the blue-leaved *Hosta* 'Halcyon'.

Ground-cover with interestingly shaped foliage is more valuable than the kind simply grown for flowers. One group that combines both features is the herbaceous geraniums. These have delicately cut palmate leaves and dish-shaped blooms. Those with white, blue, or violet-shaded flowers are preferable to those with pink, cerise, or magenta flowers, which may be too prominent among the

with that of poor dry soil, but two geraniums survive well: the near-evergreen G. x oxonianum 'Wargrave Pink' and the glossy-leaved G. nodosum, which produces subtle pale purple-pink blooms. Given a little more moisture, the white-flowered G. macrorrhizum 'Album' can also be tried. Other ground cover for dry shade includes ivies such as Hedera colchica 'Dentata', which has trails of large glossy leaves, the wavy-leaved H. helix 'Green Ripple', and the gray-and-white marbled 'Glacier'. Evergreen Iris foetidissima makes spreading clumps of narrow foliage and seeds readily. It looks good in combination with ivy and with wood spurge (Euphorbia amygdaloides var. robbiae).

To fill in around and beneath established shrubbery, the lesser periwinkle (Vinca minor) is useful. It is a creeping evergreen for sun or shade, though not for terribly dry soil. Choose plain-green-leaved cultivars with blue, purple, or white flowers in spring. Another good low filler is the dwarf fern-leaved bamboo (Pleioblastus pygmaeus).

quieter plantings of the Zen garden. Try the popular 'Johnson's Blue', the violet-purple G. wlassovianum, or the violet-blue flowered G. himalayense 'Gravetye'. All do well in either sun or light shade and prefer moisture-retentive soil.

It can be tricky to establish ground cover under trees where the problem of shade is combined

Next to boardwalks, decks, and stone paths, try swathes of Japanese silver grass (Miscanthus sinensis); the plain green, shorter-growing cultivars like 'Kleine Fontäne' have wonderful curling tassellike flowers. The evergreen lily turf (Liriope muscari) and forms of the tufted hair grass (Deschampsia caespitosa) also look good.

above: *The Japanese hakone grass is an ideal partner for blue-leaved hostas. Textural contrast between blocks of plants creates interest.*

Certain evergreen shrubs and conifers, including many junipers and several of the red-berried cotoneasters, make excellent low ground cover.

Trees

Whether evergreen or deciduous, small, elegantly shaped trees are the most suitable for the Zen garden. They provide structure, and can also create seasonal highlights.

One group long associated with Japanese gardens are the Japanese maples (*Acer palmatum* and *A.p.* var *dissectum* cultivars), the latter having more finely cut foliage. These do best in sheltered light shade, on fertile, moisture-retentive loam. They range from almost prostrate-growing shrubs to shrubs or small trees with arching or upright branches. Acers are renowned for their spectacular fall leaf coloring, and *A. p.* 'Sango-kaku' is famed for its bright coral-red stems. The sumac (*Rhus typhina*) also has excellent fall color and develops a very pleasing winter profile after a few years. Cultivars such as *R.* x *pulvinata* Autumn Lace Group have finely cut leaflets to rival the Japanese maples.

Japanese cherries are generally too flamboyant for the Zen garden, but the fall-flowering *Prunus* x *subhirtella* 'Autumnalis Rosea' is an exception. It flowers on and off through fall and winter during mild spells. The Japanese apricot (*Prunus mume*) is also recommended for its delicate winter blossom. The pink-flowered cultivar 'Beni-chidori' and white-flowered 'Omoi-no-mama' are both fragrant. The spring-flowering ornamental plums such as the

above: The sumac has an architectural profile and is best used as a specimen. Its glowing fall color rivals that of the maples.

white-flowered *Prunus cerasifera* are suitable for the Zen garden, but avoid the purple-leaved forms. Though not so traditional, some of the crab apples could also be used to emphasize the spring season, and many also have ornamental fruits in fall. The Japanese crab (*Malus floribunda*) is particularly delicate-looking and makes a small weeping tree with crimson buds that open to palest pink flowers, with small red and yellow fruits.

The hollies (*Ilex aquifolium*, *Ilex* x *altaclerensis*, and cultivars) make fine evergreen trees; their size can be controlled by pruning. Happy in sun or shade, they will stand quite a lot of exposure once established. Female cultivars sometimes produce crops of berries. Equally tough, happy on heavy clay, and more reliable for fruit production are the evergreen cotoneasters *C. salicifolius* 'Exburyensis' and 'Rothschildianus.' Both have yellow berries and

Although most commonly associated with Australia, several of the eucalyptus would look at home in a contemporary Zen design. Try the evergreen *E. pauciflora subsp. niphophila* grown as a multi-stemmed tree. The peeling bark in gray, green, and cream gives a patchwork effect like snakeskin.

above: *The pattern and texture of tree bark makes a valuable contribution to the garden in winter.* Left to right: Stewartia pseudocamellia, Acer griseum, *and* Acer crataegi folium *'Veitchii'*.

willow-shaped leaves. The red-berried 'Pendulus' is usually grafted to make a small weeping tree.

A small evergreen with beautiful shredded bark is the strawberry tree (*Arbutus unedo*). For even brighter, cinnamon-colored bark, grow the hybrid *A. x andrachnoides*. A compact tree that comes into its own in winter, *Acer griseum* also has peeling cinnamon-colored bark.

Trees with a delicate pinnate leaf lighten heavier evergreen plantings. For an effect like a pool of sunlight among dark evergreens, plant the honey locust (*Gleditsia triacanthos* 'Sunburst'). The dainty pink-berried *Sorbus vilmorinii* has similar foliage.

Small flowering trees include dogwoods (*Cornus kousa*), which have large white bracts in early summer. Unlike its showy flowered cousins, *Cornus mas* is happy on limy soils and has tiny yellow flowers on bare branches in late winter followed by red fruit. Several of the small magnolias can also work well in the Zen garden.

Evergreens

When thinking of evergreens for the Japanese garden, those that first spring to mind include rhododendrons and evergreen azaleas, pieris, camellia, and the mountain laurel (Kalmia latifolia). These all favor some shade and shelter and lime-free soil, so make sure you have the right conditions before planting.

By planting different varieties, you can have camellia flowers from fall through till spring. Some are low-growing, others are bushy or tall and upright. Colors range from creamy-white through pink to shades of red. There are singles and doubles, some of which have an exquisite sculptural beauty. Avoid positions in early-morning sun, which can damage the flowers after frost.

Pieris include neat dwarfs through to large spreading shrubs and are noted for their brilliantly colored spring leaf growth. Over winter many have ornamental tassels of flower buds; in spring they open to pale pink or white bell-shaped blooms. Rhododendron and azaleas hybrids often have large showy blooms; buy the plant in bloom so you can see the effect before planting. Mountain laurel is more delicate—this elegant shrub has glossy leaves and in early summer carries clusters of pink blooms that look like tiny parasols.

Evergreens that tolerate alkaline soils include spotted laurel (*Aucuba japonica*), a handsome shrub with subtle golden speckling that can stand fairly dense shade. Avoid heavily variegated forms like 'Crotonifolia', which are too bright for the Zen garden. The Mexican orange blossom (*Choisya ternata*) is also tolerant of shade as well as atmospheric pollution. It has attractive glossy rich-green leaves divided into a fan of leaflets and waxy white blooms, principally in early summer. The form 'Aztec' has narrow, fingerlike leaves, and 'Sundance' has soft-yellow foliage. For use as a background to smaller shrubs, and for screening, choose plants like *Elaeagnus* x *ebbingei*, which has gray-green leaves with silvery leaf backs, and *Viburnum tinus*, which has matt green leaves and domed heads of white flowers between late fall and early spring. For a more fine-textured effect and fragrance in spring, try *Osmanthus delavayi*. The pittosporums are noted for their glossy, often wavy-edged leaves and make fine specimens. Another handsome foliage plant is *Osmanthus heterophyllus* 'Goshiki', which has beautifully marbled, hollylike leaves. It looks good against *Photinia* x *fraseri* 'Red Robin', which has deep-red glossy shoot tips.

Low, rounded, or mound-forming shapes are represented by easy-to-grow shrubs including

Viburnum davidii, which has deep-green, prominently veined foliage, red leaf stalks and, if both sexes are grown, clusters of metallic-blue berries. Cultivars of little leaf box (*Buxus microphylla*) such as 'Green Pillow' naturally have dome-shaped profiles, as do forms of sweet box (*Sarcococca*), which also has clusters of tiny white headily scented flowers in winter. Both are shade lovers. For a similar effect in sun, choose Japanese holly (*Ilex crenata*) or one of its many cultivars. The small-leafed hebes could also be used in a sunny spot, but avoid those with silver

left: *Evergreens like* Osmanthus x fortunei *are grown for their foliage, which may be plain green, variegated, or tinged with color.*
below: *The evergreens provide the background structure to this garden, which will be appreciated even after the summer flowers have gone.*

or markedly glaucous foliage, which may look out of place in a Zen planting scheme. Try *Hebe cupressoides* 'Boughton Dome', *H.* 'Emerald Green', and *Hebe rakaiensis*, all of which benefit from a light annual clip in late spring.

Most conifers create a pleasing textural combination with broad-leaved shrubs. There are species and cultivars in all shapes and sizes, but the pines and cedars, with their needlelike foliage, and the junipers yield many more oriental-looking specimens. To create the right look, choose plants with an open, graceful, and irregular habit over dense compact varieties with a conical or columnar outline. Weeping plants or those with spreading branches and drooping shoot tips or branches that curve up at the ends also give a Japanese flavor.

Shrubs and Climbers

The foliage of some deciduous shrubs is almost translucent, and the sun shining through the leaves creates wonderful effects, especially with species like the smoke bush (*Cotinus coggygria*). When backlit, their rounded leaves show intricate venation. 'Grace' has larger than normal, bronze-purple-tinged foliage and exceptionally beautiful fall leaf color.

The solidity of evergreens can also be contrasted by deeply cut, almost feathery foliage, such as that of the golden cut-leaved elder *Sambucus racemosa* 'Sutherland Gold', or by very-small-leaved plants such as the variegated coralberry (*Symphoricarpos orbiculatus* 'Foliis Variegatis').

Zen celebrates all phases of growth, so buds as well as leaves and flowers are admired. Forms of *Hydrangea macrophylla* and *H. serrata* are particularly beautiful when the flower buds begin to

above: *Hardy species fuchsia with their delicate pendulous blooms make a quiet contribution to the Zen garden during summer and fall.*
right: *Clematis with small simple blooms like* Clematis alpina *'Frances Rivis' are a better choice in the Zen garden than highly bred cultivars.*

expand in early summer. Their fresh green and cream tones gradually become touched with the color of the mature flower. In cultivars like 'Preziosa' fresh blooms continue to develop from midsummer through fall. Hydrangeas age magically; in a good fall they develop myriad tones like so many faded silks. In winter, the sepia-colored skeletons remain, which may be enhanced by an icy frosting.

Most deciduous shrubs enter a quiet phase in winter, but some come into their own. Dogwoods such as *Cornus alba* 'Sibirica' with vertical laquer-red stems, and *C. stolonifera* 'Flaviramea' with bright, yellowish-green stems, look good massed on the banks of a large pond. Once the leaves open in spring, they fade into the background. The purplish-brown stems of *Rubus thibetanus* are masked by a ghostly white bloom. In winter the plant looks stunning against a dark evergreen backdrop—in summer the foliage is fernlike.

It is easy to be seduced by the beauty of a shrub in full flower, only to discover that for the rest of the year it is a formless mass of branches. Many common spring and summer flowering shrubs like *Deutzia* fall into this category. The deciduous viburnums do not suffer these drawbacks, and forms of the winter-flowering *Viburnum* x *bodnantense* have not only strong, upright growth, but also attractive, heavily-veined, red-tinged leaves.

CLIMBERS AND WALL SHRUBS

Climbers and wall shrubs are particularly valuable where space is at a premium because they can utilize the vertical surfaces. The evergreen ivies are self-clinging and take up very little room. Wall shrubs like *Pyracantha* and the spring-flowering *Chaenomeles* need support in the form of wires or trellis, and a certain amount of training to get them to fan against the surface. Unless your aim is to cover an ugly screen, make sure that only a few well-placed wall shrubs or climbers are used, to preserve the sense of space. Wisteria is an excellent climber for the Zen garden. When well-trained, the network of stems in winter is like a work of art. As the long trailing flowers appear, they need room to hang gracefully, and they are ideal plants for a large arbor. Buy grafted named cultivars; otherwise, you could wait many years for flowers.

Clematis are popular summer-flowering climbers, but avoid the large-flowered cultivars, which look unnatural. Instead try ones with bell- or lantern-shaped blooms. The vigorous yellow-flowered species *Clematis tangutica* flowers in late summer, but its ferny light green foliage makes an attractive backdrop well before then. After the blooms, the plant is covered in fluffy white whorls. In spring, the pastel-colored forms of *C. alpina* come into flower. These dainty plants can be allowed to scramble up through evergreen shrubs.

Some climbers are grown for the beauty of their foliage alone. *Parthenocissus henryana* is lovely when planted in shade, when the elegant-fingered leaves produce their best coloring—red tinged with prominent silvery venation.

The lotus (Neumbo nucifera) is the sacred symbol of Buddhism and would make a highly appropriate specimen for a large pool in the Zen garden. The large pale-pink blooms are held above the platelike leaves on sturdy stems. A tropical plant, the lotus is unsuitable for colder climes, but can be grown in a large container and lifted out in winter.

Water Plants

Water plants such as the vigorous Canadian pondweed (*Elodea canadensis*) can very quickly fill a small pond, and can be difficult to deal with once they are established. Once every year, submerged aquatics must be thinned, overgrown marginals should be divided and replanted, and floating aquatics, such as water lilies, can be reduced to keep a pleasing proportion of leaf cover to clear surface.

A newly filled pond needs time to settle before plants are introduced. Plants are best in perforated baskets lined with plastic or burlap mesh to contain the soil (special aquatic plant growing medium is best). Cover the surface with fine gravel, soak the basket, and gently lower it into position. If you do not have planting shelves, raise the baskets up on piles of brick. Combine plants with upright grassy leaves such as the yellow-banded *Scirpus* 'Zebrinus' with horizontal, spreading, or broad-leaved kinds, such as water lilies, to create a harmonious effect.

BOG GARDENS

Many bog garden plants are highly architectural including the Japanese flag (*Iris ensata*), the arum lily (*Zantedeschia aethiopica*), the royal fern (*Osmunda regalis*), and the white-flowered *Lysichiton camtshatcensis*. Some can help screen areas of water from view so different vistas open out as you walk around. Some are tender and may need protection from frost.

LILIES

In still water, plant one of the hardy water lily cultivars (*Nymphaea*). There are kinds to suit any size pool, from lakes to tiny pools in large glazed water jars—ask your local supplier to advise.

top: *With its sculptural qualities, even a single bloom of the sacred lotus* (Nelumbo nucifera) *would make a bold statement in a pool.*
above: *The curious flower spikes of golden club* (Oronitium aquaticum) *appear in spring, and contrast with the bluish-green foliage.*

Plants for Shaping

In the West we are just beginning to experiment with free-style topiary and abstract "green sculpture." Here topiary has always been quite rigidly geometric in form, but the purity of certain shapes could work well in a contemporary-style Zen landscape.

Certain small-leaved compact-growing shrubs can be clipped into the undulating organic forms or low domes typical of Japanese gardens. Many of the plants commonly used in Western topiary can be clipped into these shapes with great success, but the Japanese often use small-leaved evergeen azaleas and little-leaf box (*Buxus microphylla*), with which they create surreal, flowing landscapes. Box (*Buxus sempervirens*) and the tiny-leaved Japanese holly (*Ilex crenata*) could be used to similar effect. *Ilex vomitoria* looks similar to box and grows well in a warm humid climate.

The pea-green *Hebe rakaiensis* forms a natural dome, but the shape is even more architectural when it is clipped. Shape in late spring to remove the buds and keep the plant green all year round. Common yew (*Taxus baccata*) is ideal for large topiary. It can be clipped with architectural precision to create contemporary sculpture. Although not ideal for creating crisp shapes, *Osmanthus delavayi* will also take light clipping. In mild areas you can shape sweet bay (*Laurus nobilis*), and a similar effect can be achieved with the glossy-leaved Portugal laurel (*Prunus lusitanica*). *Viburnum*

tinus may also be shaped, though you would need to clip off the buds to prevent flowering.

Apart from undulating shapes, you can create cloud topiary, a very oriental-looking plant sculpture.

above: *In Zen, attention to form and texture is paramount. This unusual mosaic of clipped box creates a striking image.*

This consists of a single or multi-stemmed shrub in which all the side shoots and foliage are restricted to rounded heads or domed plates at the ends of the branches. Cloud topiary needs careful placing for the shape to be appreciated.

Perennials and Bulbs

The best kinds of herbaceous perennials for the Zen garden are those with attractive foliage, sculptural blooms, and no need for support or frequent division. The winter- and spring-flowering hellebores such as *Helleborus argutifolius* and cultivars of *H. orientalis* are ideal Zen plants for the shade or woodland garden. Another group displaying all the right attributes are the shorter peonies with single or semi-double blooms.

New shoots arising in spring may be colored a rich mahogany red, and the lobed leaves make a fine clump above which the single or semi-double blooms appear. Colors range from pure white and yellow to pinks and reds. The soft-yellow-flowered *Paeonia mlokosewitchii* starts the flowering season early, flowering in spring, but most bloom in early summer. They thrive if left undisturbed in a sunny, well-drained spot.

Day lilies (*Hemerocallis*) also work well in the Zen garden, especially the dainty species and small-flowered hybrids like 'Golden Chimes' and 'Corky', both of which have an abundance of yellow blooms. There are many hybrids in all colors except blue. The foliage of the day lily comes through as bright acid-green tufts in spring. It expands to form clumps of green, ribbonlike leaves, which, like ornamental grasses and sedges, look good with broad-bladed hostas. Day lilies are adaptable and cope with dappled shade. They will thrive on the edges of the bog garden as well as in drier spots.

The iris has a strong association with Japanese gardens. One of the most natural-looking and easy to please is *Iris sibirica* and its cultivars. They thrive in a sunny spot with moisture-retentive soil. They have very narrow leaves forming an upright clump, and the slender stems carry the blue, purple, or white butterfly blooms in early summer.

Although not traditionally associated with Eastern style, the smaller plain yellow or cream-flowered *Kniphofia* cultivars would be appropriate in the contemporary Zen garden, especially coming up in swathes through gravel. In a different color range entirely, the evergreen penstemons would also fit in easily, and would add color from midsummer through fall to a planting of spring-flowering evergreens, for example. Shades range from deep purple to crimson red, pink, and white. Avoid the large-leaved varieties, which are less hardy and less elegant, and stay with cultivars that have narrow, almost willowlike leaves.

above left: Lilies with an Oriental character look good in the Zen garden, adding seasonal color between permanent plantings.
*above right: The stripes on the leaves of this tall columnar grass (*Miscanthus sinensis* 'Zebrinus') create the effect of dappled light.*

For a striking combination of handsome foliage and flower, try *Acanthus spinosus*. The deeply cut leaves are dark green and glossy, and the rosettes are among the first to emerge in spring. The tall mauve flower spikes with long-lasting spiny bracts appear in late summer, and the whole plant is so striking that it can easily stand alone. Most of the spurges (*Euphorbia*), such as *Euphorbia characias* subsp. *wulfenii,* have attractive foliage and unusual flowers, and create a modern feel. For an injection of hot color, try *Euphorbia grifithii* 'Fireglow', which flowers in early summer, or 'Dixter'.

BULBS

Bulbs create seasonal highlights throughout the year. For spring, plant drifts of low-growing bulbs, including dwarf forms of daffodil, all of which die down after flowering and rarely need lifting and dividing. With the exception of sun-loving crocus, most of these early bulbs are happy in sun or shade. Early summer is the season for the drumstick-headed ornamental onions (*Allium*), which come in shades of purple. The silvery-lilac heads of *Allium christophii* are larger than some of the taller-growing alliums and their long-lasting seed heads are a feature for months. Many lilies have an Oriental look, and work well in the summer garden coming up through lower plantings. In fall *Nerine* and fall-flowering crocus appear unexpectedly.

Mosses and Ferns

Moss will colonize moist, shaded soil and rock of its own accord. The microscopic spores blow in the wind and settle by chance. Some moss species are restricted to quite specific habitats, so it is inadvisable, as well as potentially damaging to the environment, to dig up moss clumps for use in your garden.

If conditions are not ideal for the growth of mosses, try one of the many creeping or cushion-forming alpines, such as the mossy saxifrages. As the name implies, they form carpets of mosslike foliage, but the effect is temporarily marred by the appearance of white, pink, or red starry blooms. Another alternative is the non-flowering form of chamomile (*Chamaemelum nobile* 'Treneague'), which has fresh green, fruitily aromatic growth. Creeping thymes are also worth trying, although again, tiny flowers are produced at certain times of the year. *Cotoneaster microphyllus* var. *thymifolius* (syn. *C. linearifolius*) is an unusual member of this common genus; it forms a close evergreen carpet of minute leaves, and the branches cling to the ground and follow every contour to give an interesting effect and the appearance of age.

Mind-your-own-business or baby's tears (*Soleirolia soleirolii*) is another good moss mimic. Normally sold as a houseplant with domed growth, in the garden the plant forms a thin layer of tiny filmy leaves. Given shade and moisture, it will colonize rocks and bare earth. The creeping mint (*Mentha requienii*) enjoys similar conditions and releases a wonderful aroma when trodden upon. Both plants look effective weaving in between cobblestones around the edge of a natural pool. If you combine a selection of these plants, even in a sunny site you can create a reasonable facsimile of a moss garden.

FERNS

Natural partners for moss, ferns conjure up images of shady woodland. But some ferns can be grown in any shady spot which has a degree of moisture—a narrow bed, along a shady wall, or in a dry rock garden beneath trees. There are many kinds of ferns, some more demanding than others, and forms have proliferated in horticulture because of the tendency that ferns have to "sport," or spontaneously change, in the wild.

The scaly male fern (*Dryopteris felix-mas*) is tolerant of fairly dry shade and makes the typical shuttlecock of fronds. It has several interesting forms with more elaborate leaf design. *Dryopteris erythrosora* is another attractive species. The lady fern (*Athyrium felix-femina*) has daintier fronds and requires a humous-rich, moisture-retentive soil.

Some ferns are evergreen, though it is advisable to cut off the old fronds just as the new ones are beginning to unfurl. Two that are readily available are the soft shield fern (*Polystichum setiferum*) and hard shield ferns (*P. aculeatus*). The fronds of the hard shield fern are compact, relatively narrow, and unusually glossy. Common polypody (*Polypodium vulgare*) is also evergreen and can be planted between rocks or in a dry stone wall, mimicking the way it is often seen growing in the wild.

above: *In spring, young fern crosiers unfurl slowly and gracefully, finally expanding into the familiar lacy fronds.*

left: *The shuttlecock formation of ferns like* Matteuccia *and* Dryopteris *is highly architectural and can be used to great effect.*

Index

Acknowledgments

The publisher would like to thank the following for supplying the illustrations:

Clive Nichols Garden Pictures: pp. bottom right cover (designer Jim Reynolds), 7 (Hannah Peschar Gallery), 9 (Hiroshi Nanamori, Chelsea 96), 15 (Netherfield Herb Garden), 32 (J Dowle & Kninomiya, Chelsea), 51, 54 (Little Coopers, Hampshire), 60, (Denmans/John Brookes), 61 (Huntingdon Botanical Gardens), 72 (designer Christopher Bradley-Hole), 77 (J Dowle & Kninomiya, Chelsea), 79 (Trevyn McDowell), 81 (Gordon White, Austin,

Texas), top left cover and 85 (Spidergarden.com/Chelsea), 89, 114 (top left), 117 (designer Sarah Hammond)

John Glover Photography: pp. 1, 2, 12, 14, 23, 27, 33, 38, 41, 44, 46, 50, 56, 71, 74, 91, 92, 93, 94, 98, 99, 102, 105, 106, 107, 108, 111, 113, 120 (both)

Harpur Garden Library: pp. top right cover, 17 (Mr and Mrs Lunn, Vancouver), 18-19, 24, 28 (Terry Welch, Seattle), 31, 42, 49 (designer Isabelle C Greene), 52, 62, 67, 68 (designer Oehme & Van Sweden, Washington DC)

Christian Williams: pp. 5, 43, 80, 112

Sunniva Harte pp. 22, 35, 36, 37, 39, 45, 47, 65, 70, 125

Derek St Romaine Photography: pp. back cover, bottom left cover, 11, 13, 22, 58, 95, 122, 124

Jenny Hendy: pp. 26, 75, 82

Coral Mula: pp. 55, 59, 64, 66, 76, 76, 83

David and Charles: pp. 69 (PL Linearis), 123

Justyn Willsmore: pp. 86, 103, 104, 114 (right), 115 (both), 116, 118, 119

Diana Poole: p 121